YOUR CABIN IN THE WOODS

*A Compilation
of Cabin Plans and Philosophy for
Discovering Life in the
Great Out Doors*

by

Conrad Meinecke

BONANZA BOOKS

NEW YORK

This book was originally published in 1945.
Special material copyright © MCMLXXIX by Crown Publishers, Inc.
All rights reserved.
This edition is published by Bonanza Books,
a division of Crown Publishers, Inc.
   b c d e f g h
BONANZA 1979 EDITION
Manufactured in the United States of America

Library of Congress Cataloging in Publication Data
Meinecke, Conrad E.
   Your cabin in the woods.
   Reprint of the 1945 ed. published by Foster & Stewart,
Buffalo; with new introd.
   1. Log cabins. 2. Architecture, Domestic—Designs
and plans. 3. Outdoor life. I. Title.
NA8470.M4   1979   728'.7   79-14087
ISBN 0-517-26933-3

Dedicated to my lovely

Mother

Who loved life; who could take it with courage; who loved and understood primitive living; who by the hard way learned to love and appreciate a cabin in the woods; who spent her early life in a cabin in a lonely woods and loved it, but who did not live long enough for me to satisfy the realization of her later dreams—a "Cabin in the woods."

God bless her buoyant soul.

Conrad E. Meinecke

Foreword to the 1979 Edition

Thoreau said that if an emergency struck, a man should be able to leave his home with nothing more than the clothes on his back without feeling that he had left anything behind. This implies a self-sufficiency that is nearly impossible to attain in modern society. In this age of mechanization there is little that we do for ourselves. Technology, which has brought so many things to such a high level, has also burdened us with countless material things that we regard as necessities. We take it for granted that every family will have a television, stereo system, automobile, and numerous household appliances.

Not surprisingly, one of the prevailing dreams of our time is that of the return to the land, to the simple life. But it need not be merely a dream. In *Your Cabin in the Woods,* Conrad Meinecke gives very clear step-by-step instructions on how anyone can build one of many different small cabins that will house any number of people comfortably. The well detailed plans he gives include functional plumbing and heating.

More than this, though, Meinecke creates an atmosphere of peacefulness and practicability. He quietly exhorts us to consider the benefits to be derived from spending a good deal of time with nature, away from the cares and concerns of city life. He tells us in a

conversational and personal way how to prepare ourselves for life in the woods, explaining how to overcome our fears of nature, and how we can find endless
entertainment and satisfaction from the richness of
day-to-day communion with nature.

Meinecke also advocates wilderness life as the
best way to achieve communion with other people.
Helping one another with simple chores, watching
over each other's homes, sharing needs like food and
firewood, simple fellowship: these are the things that
make for true community spirit. And in the simple
rustic life these things emerge more clearly as our
true concerns.

Meinecke thinks of America as the land of the
free, and he recognizes that freedom from material care
is as important as freedom from tyranny. He echoes the
spirit of the pioneers in his love of mankind, his delight
in life's simple pleasures, and his passion for the great
outdoors. Such a spirit is certainly as important today
as it was 200 years ago.

SOLOMON J. SCHEPPS

Foreword

First of all, Conrad Meinecke's Cabin in the Woods is a cabin not made with hands; it is eternal in the heaven of his mind. He has roamed the Rockies, tramped the Balkans, lived in adobe, bedded down in the desert of restless sands, but always he comes back to his true love —a cabin in the woods. He has built thirty-two cabins and fireplaces in the Rockies and in Canada and now has six cabins scattered about in the Western Hemisphere.

From his artist, linguistic father who at ninety-three could still do a hand-stand, and from his Scotch-Swiss mother who combined a practical, pioneering type of thinking with a high degree of spirituality, he inherited a some-thing in his genes that defies imprisoning in words. He is a lean, tough specimen illuminated by a quenchless inner fire of spirituality. His tireless energy, his buoyancy, and strange to say, his quietness of spirit, spring from his com-munion with forms, visible and invisible, of the great out-of-doors. At sometime, like his grand old father, he has had a draught from the fabled fountain of Immortal Youth. He is fortunate in his ancestry—the genes somehow "blended" just right. Then in his boyhood his Indian mentor, "Neck-tie Jim," taught him how to listen when on the other side of the world the "red gods" were calling him to help them make their "medecin."

Curiously enough, with this idealism, this high spirituality, this understanding love of the inner meaning of life, he combines a Yankee, practical ingenuity. He is the best cook that ever concocted a meal for me in the wilderness. He "swings a mean skillet." If he says, "build your fireplace so and so," do it. And when you have done it, you can stretch your moccasined feet to the fire and have no smoke in your eyes. Build your cabin the way he tells you and you will have a joy forever, partly because you built it and partly because it "belongs" to the particular spot of its own earth, partly because it's as handy as a pocket in a shirt, and then, too, because it's easy on your income.

This man tramps all over the earth and when he settles down, builds himself a "nest" on the end of a twig as practical and as intriguing as that of the Baltimore oriole. Somehow he has so much—maybe it is because he is always giving it away.

From being a successful young man in business affairs, he turned to working with and for men and boys. Somehow he has in his spiritual heritage and in his ripening wisdom, the blessedness of sharing. From his "Cabin in the Woods," you can learn how to fashion *your* cabin, but more, you may become more fit to live in a "house not made with hands, eternal in the heavens."

Elbert K. Fretwell
Chief Scout Executive
Boy Scouts of America

CONTENTS AND ILLUSTRATIONS

Lifting the Latch

THERE is nothing unusual in these pages. There is little that I may claim as original. Some of the material here treated is as old as time. Many friends and books have contributed to its contents. My thirty years of outdoor experience and cabin building may, however, save the reader much of the "trial and error" method when he builds his "Cabin-in-the-Woods."

I have attempted most of all to help build an attitude of mind toward the Great Outdoors —an appreciation of simple living. I want to influence both men and women toward the belief and confidence that they are "masters of their destiny" if they can stay within the realm of their own potentialities; if they can find a normal "out" for their abilities in this creative field of the outdoors. Indeed they can be "master builders" in the best sense. Resourcefulness, initiative and a love for things natural—these are the values which may give us a new concept of simple living in a very complicated and mechanical civilization.

You, too, can build a "Cabin-in-the-Woods." Cabin-building is fun; is satisfying, and here you can learn to be a master builder instead of just a helper. Detailed and minute description of every step in building a cabin can prove confusing and discouraging to the novice. If you wish to study beyond the information here given, you will find ample help in the reference reading or in your public library. You will naturally go through that period of experimentation which is the "trial and error" method. Your trials, however, need not be crowded with too many errors.

I am counting on that great American quality, "horse sense." So go to it, Mr. Cabin-Builder. Keep in mind you are going to build a better and bigger cabin some day. In your first experiment, fortified by all the descriptive material you can understand and assimilate, wade in and go to work. Do it courageously and don't you dare apologize for mistakes made. You won't make the same mistake twice. Besides building your first cabin, you will absorb techniques so essential—a combination of theory and practice.

In fireplace building the feel of a trowel in your hand; the skill of "slinging the mud," to recognize cement, sand and water mixed to the right consistency and what it means to "sweeten" or "temper" the mixture—all these will find their rightful places and give you skills. They do not come from books alone.

Again, the art of pulling a cross-cut saw; the swinging of the axe and the making of the chips to fly; the choice of axe handle that fits your grip and your height—these skills we develop through the doing.

This book is written for those who would "revert back to the land"—land near your city home—five, ten or thirty miles—a place that can be used week-ends and on vacations; indeed, throughout the year. It is written, too, for the "poor" man, that is, the man not rich in worldly goods but rich in dreams, imagination, resourcefulness and a willingness to make it happen.

BLESS those folks who can wrest from the earth its richness, its wealth, its natural resources and find its peace. That is our God-given right.

Acknowledgments

HOW can I adequately pay tribute to all who have contributed to this book? I would be at a loss to mention all the men, women, and books that have influenced my life and my thinking on this subject, "The Great Outdoors."

Lest I should slight any one, lest I should over or under estimate any one's particular contribution, I have decided to here acknowledge "Necktie Jim," the Indian who represents in a more or less degree all contributors to this book.

I am sure you will like Necktie Jim. I met him when I was a boy. My parents trusted him. He was not a great Indian Chief—just a plain Winnebago Indian—tall, stalwart, proud. He wore a loin cloth and a modern necktie; sometimes slacks or overalls. It might seem ludicrous to us, but he was serious and wore his necktie consistently and with dignity.

I camped with Necktie Jim when I was twelve years old. Our equipment was two blankets, a knife and a small hatchet. I carried my own duffel. Our food was a small sack of flour or cornmeal, salt and a bit of bear grease.

We went on one, two or three-day treks through the deep forests of northern Wisconsin—through swamp and highlands.

One day as we sat beside our campfire cooking our meal, he stood up, listened, came back and sat down. Suddenly he stood up again and listened. Finally he said, "White man coming." Sure enough, soon a man came stalking by our camp. I asked Necktie Jim, "How did you know some one was coming?" To which he replied, "Crow call. Squirrel scold. White man make noise."

In the marshes we gathered roots which contributed to our balanced diet. We snared bullfrogs and had broiled froglegs for dinner. We caught trout with a pronged stick. We caught porcupine—the last resort for the starving Indian when the snow is deep.

When the night grew cold and one blanket was not enough, we moved nearer the embers of our campfire and slept with our backs to the warm coals . . . and slept well.

Most of all Necktie Jim shared with me the joy of living happily out-of-doors. I have found throughout these years a "re-charging" when I return to the woods and an ever present urge to be a part of the outdoors whenever the occasion permits.   I learned, too, that nature is rich in abundance and will supply our daily needs. "Life, liberty and the pursuit of happiness" has its roots down deep in the soil of this great American Outdoors.

Conrad E. Meinecke

Your Cabin in the Woods

Your Cabin-in-the-Woods

SO you are another lover of the out-of-doors who desires a cabin or shelter in the woods! I salute you. I understand you. I know your kind. You carry the spirit of our ancestors. The spirit of the "Great Out Doors." The first letters of these three words spell "G O D." There is an irresistible force in the great outdoors——the very soul of America. This is as it should be.

3

And so from the start let me chat with you in a very personal way. Let's take each other at face value. I picture you as sitting on a log, dressed in colorful outdoor togs while I am nestled against the notch in a big tree, hugging my knees—eager to talk it over. I feel somehow we both want this cabin to represent our own handicraft. It must be cozy, equipped with comforts—beds, cots or bunks according to our own fancy. It must be made bright and warm with a glowing fireplace. It must have rustic furniture and at least a five-foot bookshelf of our own choice books. Old-fashioned kerosene lamps again become a luxury as they throw their soft flickering shadows.

The howling wind, the sleet driving with an impact against our tightly-built cabin will only add to the security and snugness inside. Add another log to the fire. Readjust the cushions and let the world go by. This is life— with a friend who understands. Snugness and security in our Cabin-in-the-Woods, be it sunshine or tempest. This is life.

Because we are used to city houses with a multiplicity of household duties, our Cabin-in-the-Woods should be built where there is quiet; where housework can be reduced to a minimum; where our time may be given over to the perusal of a few chosen books; where reflection may have its full sway; where one may be carefree in the great outdoors. Here, for a brief spell, we may find in its very fullness, "Life, liberty and the pursuit of happiness."

So now, "Partner-on-the-log" opposite, let us plan our Cabin-in-the-Woods. Which shall it be—a log cabin or a frame building? There really is not much difference in the planning.

First of all, let us not be too concerned about the whole venture. The cost of land need not be prohibitive. The problem of the distance from town can be solved. Building costs, how to get logs, transportation, reforestation, trails and trail markers, gateways and fences, sanitation, lighting, lamps, and many other questions will be discussed in the following pages. If the desire is there and the will to see it through, the building of your Cabin-in-the-Woods will be fun. Resourcefulness and initiative will meet the challenge. Most important of all, let us take our time. Let us plan carefully. Let us get as much enjoyment in the building as in the finished cabin.

A cabin and campsite in the woods, after all, should never be finished, for when there is nothing new to develop or nothing to be added, there will be little fun.

Start Making Notes

In the original privately printed edition of this book, ample margins and blank pages afforded room for personal notes, plans, sketches, photos and clippings; also for signatures of friends who helped plan or build the cabin in the woods.

In this edition most of the blank pages had to be omitted, but you will find other open spots for making notes. Use them, from the start, to collect material for your cabin-building program. They will not only prove invaluable later, but you will make this book truly yours, expressing your own individuality, and honoring the author by permitting him to collaborate with you in producing your own exclusive volume—"YOUR Cabin-in-the-Woods."

Important note to the 1979 edition: Since this book was originally published in 1945, the dollar figures cited should be revised to today's prices.

Plan Wisely and You Plan for the Future

ABOVE all things, let us not plan too quickly, build hurriedly or lay out our grounds haphazardly. Let us not be concerned if we do not accomplish this in a week or a month, or even in a year. I knew a man who built a shack in the woods. It was little better than a woodshed. The next year he needed another room so he tacked a lean-to on one side. Then he added another and another. The roof looked like an ocean of waves. When he got through his place looked like a big sprawling shack. No general floor level—no plan; low ceilings, poor ventilation. What a mess. He did not plan wisely. Like Topsy, "It just growed." He is the kind of fellow who says, "If I were to do it again, I'd do so and so."

7

So, Mr. Cabin-builder, I say plan wisely. Spend a summer on your site in a tent before you build. Study the air currents that flow down the hills; the prevailing winds; the landscape and vista you want to develop. Do you prefer sunrise to sunset? If you do not enjoy sunrise, then set your cabin so the morning sun will not disturb your sleep. You may enjoy the sunset from your porch or big window. Where are the noises from highways and how can you plant trees to blot out ugly views or even some of the noise?

Lastly, blueprint your newly acquired playground. Pace it off at two-hundred feet intervals, both ways. Do this if you have an acre or one hundred acres. Record on your field notes what you find—springs, gullies, kinds of trees, bushes, rocks, ground erosion and if you find the latter, seek advice on what to plant to overcome this hazard.

You will discover more natural resources and materials which you can use later and you will know where to find them when you need them. On your master blueprint locate your yearly tree plantings, roadways, trails, springs, dates of events, et cetera. It will prove a story-book of your Cabin-in-the-Woods.

Who Knows ?

This may be

Your future

Home

May I now invite you to deeper thought in your planning? Who knows what ten years from now will hold for you. You may consider retirement and make your future home in this spot of your dreams. Then again, you may turn farmer on a small scale—chickens, perhaps a pig, a cow and a garden spot. Start a beehive or two—honey is stored in the flowers about your place. Don't close your mind to the thought. You may discover your greatest contentment and happiness, also skills and aptitudes which you did not know you had. That's what our pioneer fathers did. It was about their only choice in those days.

This idea may provide a means of escape from the reality and tension of city life. It may prove a step forward and upward in the fulfillment of your life's ambitions.

Life, after all, need not necessarily be measured in accomplishment of wealth, great achievement, nor by standards of public opinion. If you have a partner who thinks likewise and is not regimented by conventional thinking, then I say, Mr. Cabin-Builder, lay your plans boldly—whether you go to the wilds of Africa, to the South Sea Islands, or to your cabin in the woods—so long as you go you may find life, liberty and ultimate happiness.

A Cure for Restlessness

Your Cabin-in-the-Woods can be a perfect cure for restlessness. If you are restless today, you may be even more restless ten years from now, unless you do something about it now. Life brings increasing cares. So going to your dream-spot month after month, year in and year out, you will experience a re-charging, a rehabilitation, a re-creating.

Your Cabin-in-the-Woods should always present enough challenge to keep you constantly adding to its loveliness. In this way after each visit you will return to your city life rested, stronger, revived.

It is obvious then that we should take our time—months, years, predicating our building on long-term planning.

Take full enjoyment in the building. Take time out to rest. Most city folks seem always to rush things through. Why? Lay off until tomorrow. Take an afternoon nap. Stop the clock for the week-end. Get off to an early start in the cool of tomorrow morning. You may be crowded in your work in town, but this should be your rest-cure, your re-creating. Don't spoil it by city-driving standards. Set your own pattern. You will be rewarded with increasing peace of mind from year to year.

Again, I say, here is a perfect cure for restlessness.

One Room
or Seven

One Room or Seven?

And now for a word about the size of the cabin itself. Have you in the back of your head some notion of a three, five or seven-room building? You have a big family? You need guest rooms?

THE FAMILY CAMP—
SUMMER AND WINTER

I HAVE in my own cabin-site accommodations for fourteen people. But they are not all in one building. I, too, had many to provide for, but I started simply some twenty years ago with a plan.

First we built a large living room, eighteen by twenty-four feet—with a good foundation, large windows; in fact one window with forty-nine panes in it measured eight feet wide by six and one-half feet high and afforded a five-mile view across the valley.

We included a big fireplace. Later we added a spacious porch on two sides. On a third side we added a kitchen and a combination wash and dressing room. No bath. The shower was placed under the porch. The north end of the porch supplied what we called the "master bedroom"—twin beds. The porch today is richly enclosed with woodbine.

As our needs grew we added nine by twelve foot tents—two beds in each, a locker, chairs, et cetera. Finally there were four tents added and we were set for the summers. With this arrangement there was freedom for every one— more independence and plenty of privacy. One member of the party could retire or take an afternoon nap while the rest of the group would be free to play without concern about those who wanted quiet.

This, of course, did not take care of our winter needs. But as one of the tents had served its time, we replaced it with a lovely one-room bedroom cabin with a large porch. It was finished with pine board, included clothes closet, washstand and a large fireplace. This bedroom cabin which is our latest addition, not more than two hundred feet away from our main living room cabin, is nestled on the hillside and is the envy of every one who sees it. In summer we sleep on the screened-in porch.

Thus we have built a seven-room house— each room with an outlook on four sides, plenty of ventilation, privacy—all with real comfort.

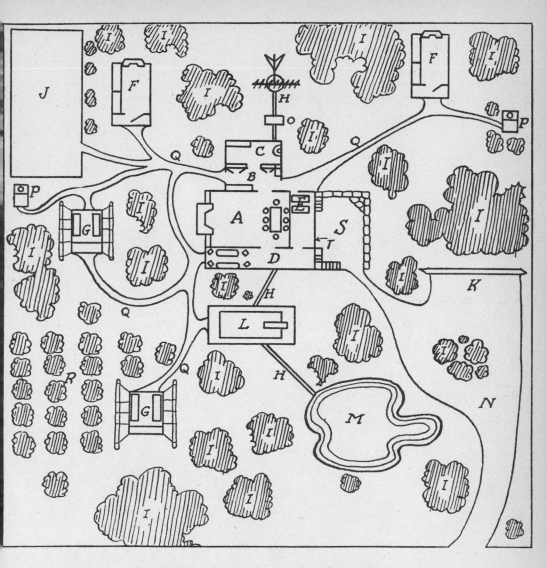

LEGEND OF FAMILY CAMP GROUNDS

A.	Main Living Room	K.	Parking Lot
B.	Kitchen	L.	Swimming Pool 9 by 15 feet
C.	Wash and Storeroom	M.	Lily Pond
D.	Veranda	N.	Driveway
E.	"Master Bedroom" on Porch	O.	Hot Water Heater
F.	Guest Cabin	P.	"Johnnie"
G.	Guest Tent	Q.	Trails
H.	Windmill and Water System	R.	Fruit Trees
I.	Shade Trees	S.	Sunken Garden - Outdoor Fireplace
J.	Tennis Court or Vegetable Plot	T.	Shower under veranda

THE FAMILY CABIN AND FLOOR PLAN

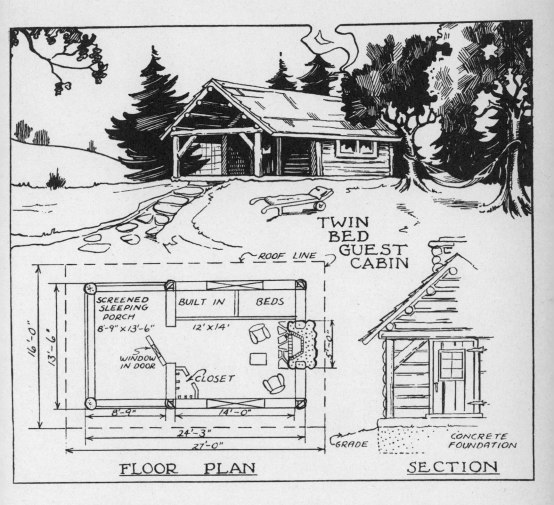

TWIN
BED
GUEST
CABIN

ROOF LINE

SCREENED
SLEEPING
PORCH
8'-9" x 13'-6"

BUILT IN   BEDS
12' X 14'

WINDOW
IN DOOR

CLOSET

16'-0"

13'-6"

8'-9"

14'-0"

24'-3"

27'-0"

FLOOR PLAN

GRADE

CONCRETE
FOUNDATION

SECTION

19

THE-FAMILY-CAMP-GUEST-TENT

TENT
FLY

THE GUEST TENT FOR TWO

A tent, fly, tent-frame and platform can
be had for about sixty dollars. With care your
bedroom tent will last about eight to ten years.
Standard nine by twelve tents cost about
twenty-five dollars—fly extra. The fly will
give you a guarantee against leaking. Also
when anchored to side posts it will keep your
tent fixed and secure against storms. The platform will give you a level floor and add dryness
and cleanliness.

Eight-ounce duck canvas, double filled, is
heavy enough for this size tent. Hang tent over
wood frame and fasten all around bottom. Guy
ropes not needed. Tent wall is two feet six
inches high. Therefore to have standing room

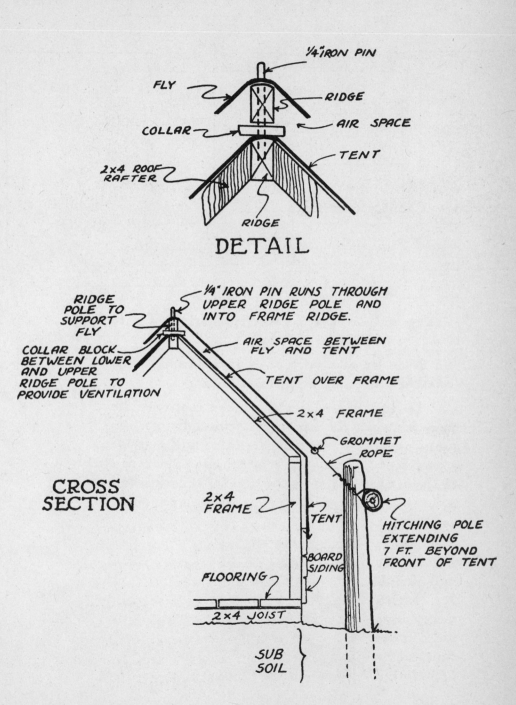

DETAIL

¼" IRON PIN
FLY
RIDGE
AIR SPACE
COLLAR
TENT
2x4 ROOF RAFTER
RIDGE

CROSS SECTION

RIDGE POLE TO SUPPORT FLY

¼" IRON PIN RUNS THROUGH UPPER RIDGE POLE AND INTO FRAME RIDGE.

COLLAR BLOCK BETWEEN LOWER AND UPPER RIDGE POLE TO PROVIDE VENTILATION

AIR SPACE BETWEEN FLY AND TENT

TENT OVER FRAME

2x4 FRAME

GROMMET ROPE

2x4 FRAME

TENT

HITCHING POLE EXTENDING 7 FT. BEYOND FRONT OF TENT

BOARD SIDING

FLOORING

2x4 JOIST

SUB SOIL

21

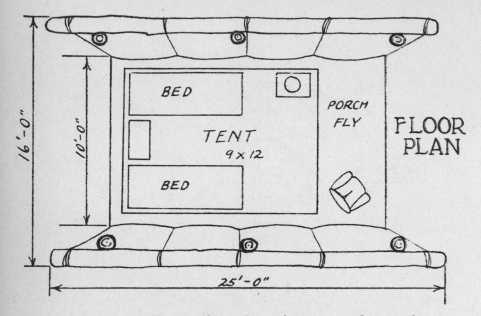

BED

TENT
9 x 12

BED

PORCH
FLY

FLOOR
PLAN

16'-0"

10'-0"

25'-0"

a frame wall is built to four feet six inches with two-foot board siding below.

Nine by twelve tent is large enough for twin beds, dresser, washstand, rug.

Tent fly, if ten feet by sixteen feet with air space between fly and tent, will help to keep your tent cool in hot weather; also will provide a four-foot porch. On warm sunny days roll up the canvas walls, let the breezes through and make the hillside part of your living quarters.

Our Window Picture Frame

The big window in our cabin resembles a
picture frame in which miles of landscape across
the valley bring nature's choicest pictures to
life. Each hour of the day brings intriguing
new vistas, changing lights and shadows.

The early morning sun lights up the sparkling lily pond below us, which in turn throws playful, mischievous lights about us. As the day wears on pastoral scenes replace the picture of the misty morning and through our "picture frame" we see the hillside dotted with lowing cattle, green fields boxed in with rail fences and lined with small trees and bushes—telling the story of the toil and accomplishment of our neighboring farmers. An occasional tall elm or maple stand as sentinels in the march of time. Far beyond "stately ships of fleecy white clouds sail majestically across the dark blue ocean of the sky" leaving one in awe, for such scenery is only painted with bold strokes by the hand of the Master Painter.

Even the sun-dial on a cloudy day seems to reflect our mood of response to nature—and so time passes on. Finally lengthening shadows; dissolving glory of eventide—night—twinkling stars and a full moon.

Whenever you look out of a window, whatever the view, try to remember that you are looking at one of God's great pictures.

There never were paintings comparable to those in the big window of our Cabin-in-the-Woods.

Cabin

Composition

ONE ROOM CABIN

Here is the perfect, yet very simplest two-man log cabin you can wish for. Low in cost and easy to build. It can be constructed as small as nine by twelve feet (inside measurement), or twelve by fourteen, fourteen by eighteen, or even larger. The larger cabin needs added structural material.

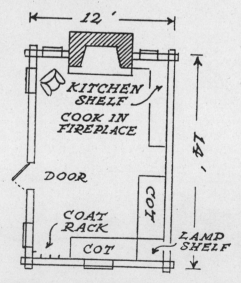

Let's discuss the nine by twelve two-man log cabin—just one room with two commodious couches, each with a view of the fireplace. A kitchenette quite complete to the right of the fireplace, two comfortable chairs and a table. It's the very essence of snugness. It can be easily ventilated at upper gables without creating a draft. Floor of flagstones.

If you have natural material on your cabin site such as logs and stones, you will only have to purchase such material as cement, boards to cover your roof, shingles, windows, nails, a bit of lumber for the inside.

VIEW FROM
FIREPLACE

TWO ROOM CABIN

This cabin has the added storm-porch and toilet room. The cabin proper is the same. The added storm-porch offers a bit more of comfort and refinement without adding much to the cost. The toilet—a slop bucket with seat and cover, also pipe vent running to outside makes this type free from odors. The bucket is emptied from time to time in the backyard toilet. It serves its best purpose for winter use, when one does not gather much enthusiasm, especially on a stormy night, to visit the backyard "Johnnie." An oil heater will keep this room comfortable. Then there is the washstand. Improvise your own supply water tank; also drain the stationary with pipe to the outside. Note, also, the neatly piled wood within the storm-porch. Nothing like having dry wood to start your fire, especially if you arrive on a stormy night. A nine by twelve cabin can be comfortably heated by the fireplace.

I know of a nine by twelve log cabin that was built for less than seventy dollars. You, too, can have an inexpensive cabin if you supply your own labor—that is, do it yourself, and if

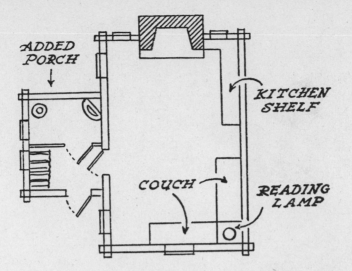

ADDED PORCH

KITCHEN SHELF

COUCH

READING LAMP

much of the natural material is on the land for the taking. A nine by twelve log cabin will require fourteen logs (seven inches average thickness) twenty-one feet long; also sixteen poles (four and a half inch average thickness) eight feet long for the roof rafters.

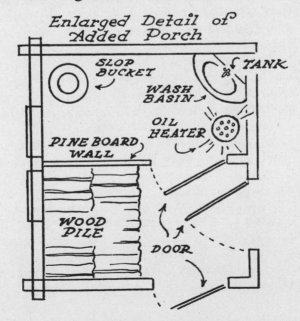

Enlarged Detail of Added Porch

SLOP BUCKET

TANK

WASH BASIN

OIL HEATER

PINE BOARD WALL

WOOD PILE

DOOR

FOUR ROOM CABIN

Now we come to the spreading idea. Obviously it would not be satisfactory if you have more than two to provide for, to build on the front and back the added rooms here suggested on a nine by twelve cabin. You may now want to build your prize cabin with living room, say fourteen by eighteen or larger. However, the nine by twelve can still enjoy a lean-to on the back by cutting a door as indicated in this floor plan. The kitchen would be small—about six by six feet, but if carefully planned with small stove, shelves, etc., it will enrich even a small cabin.

You will never have greater enjoyment out of any cabin in the woods than the nine by twelve log cabin for two. It's snug. It suggests team work. It invites consideration. It is rudely complete. It provides the perfect setting for ideal companionship. In modern slang, "It's a natural."

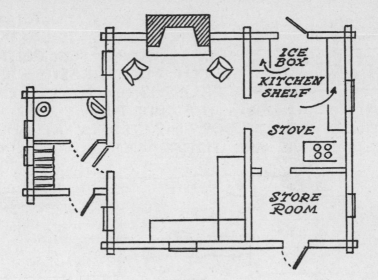

ICE
BOX

KITCHEN
SHELF

STOVE

STORE
ROOM

VIEW FROM COUCH

31

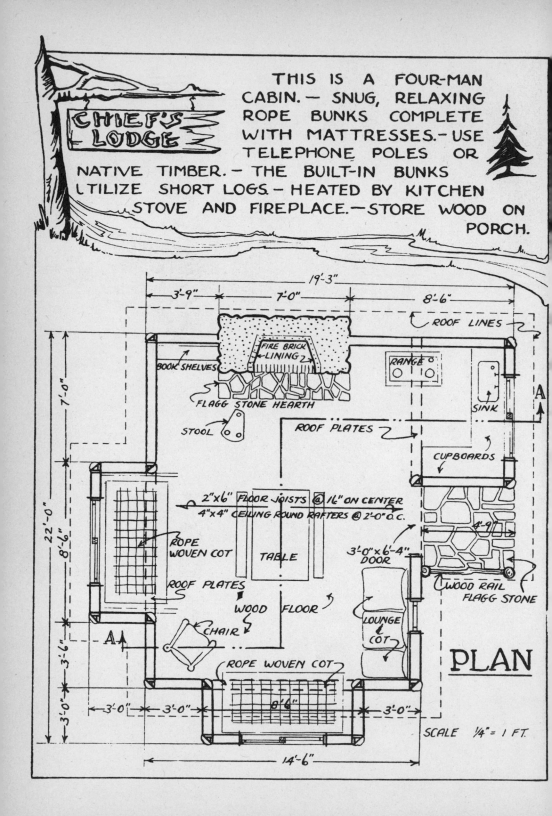

CHIEF'S LODGE

THIS IS A FOUR-MAN CABIN. — SNUG, RELAXING ROPE BUNKS COMPLETE WITH MATTRESSES. — USE TELEPHONE POLES OR NATIVE TIMBER. — THE BUILT-IN BUNKS UTILIZE SHORT LOGS. — HEATED BY KITCHEN STOVE AND FIREPLACE. — STORE WOOD ON PORCH.

19'-3"
3'-9"
7'-0"
8'-6"
ROOF LINES
BOOK SHELVES
FIRE BRICK LINING 2
RANGE
7'-0"
FLAGG STONE HEARTH
SINK
A
STOOL
ROOF PLATES
CUPBOARDS
22'-0"
8'-6"
2"x6" FLOOR JOISTS @ 16" ON CENTER
4"x4" CEILING ROUND RAFTERS @ 2'-0" O.C.
ROPE WOVEN COT
TABLE
3'-0"x6'-4" DOOR
4'-9"
ROOF PLATES
WOOD FLOOR
WOOD RAIL FLAGG STONE
3'-6"
A
CHAIR
LOUNGE & COT
3'-0"
ROPE WOVEN COT
PLAN
3'-0"
3'-0"
3'-0"
8'-6"
3'-0"
SCALE ¼" = 1 FT.
14'-6"

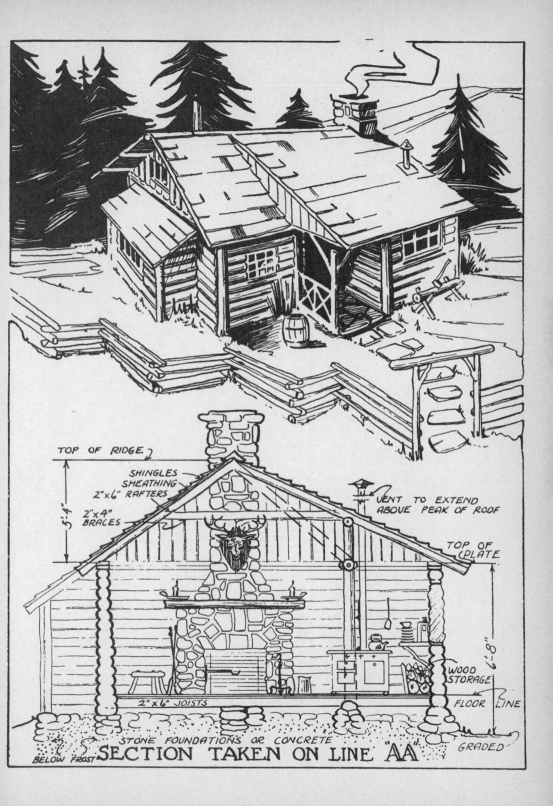

TOP OF RIDGE

SHINGLES
SHEATHING
2"x6" RAFTERS

2"x4"
BRACES

5'-4"

VENT TO EXTEND
ABOVE PEAK OF ROOF

TOP OF
PLATE

6'-8"

WOOD
STORAGE

FLOOR LINE

2"x6" JOISTS

STONE FOUNDATIONS OR CONCRETE

BELOW FROST

SECTION TAKEN ON LINE "AA"

GRADED

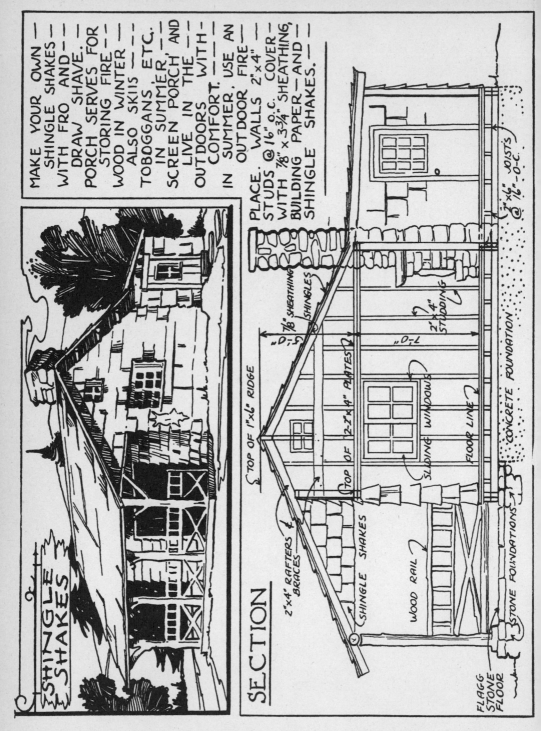

MAKE YOUR OWN — SHINGLE SHAKES — WITH FRO AND — DRAW SHAVE. — PORCH SERVES FOR — STORING FIRE — WOOD IN WINTER — ALSO SKIIS — TOBOGGANS ETC. — IN SUMMER — SCREEN PORCH, AND — LIVE IN THE — OUTDOORS WITH — COMFORT. — — IN SUMMER, USE AN — OUTDOOR FIRE —

PLACE. WALLS 2"x4" — STUDS @ 16" O.C. COVER — WITH 7/8" x 3¾" SHEATHING, — BUILDING PAPER — AND — SHINGLE SHAKES. —

SHINGLE SHAKES

SECTION

TOP OF 1"x6" RIDGE

5'-0"

7/8 SHEATHING

SHINGLES

2"x4" RAFTERS &
BRACES

2"x4" STUDDING

7'-0"

SHINGLE SHAKES

TOP OF 2-2"x4" PLATES

SLIDING WINDOWS

FLOOR LINE

WOOD RAIL

CONCRETE FOUNDATION

2"x6" JOISTS
@ 16"-O-C.

FLAGG
STONE
FLOOR

STONE FOUNDATIONS

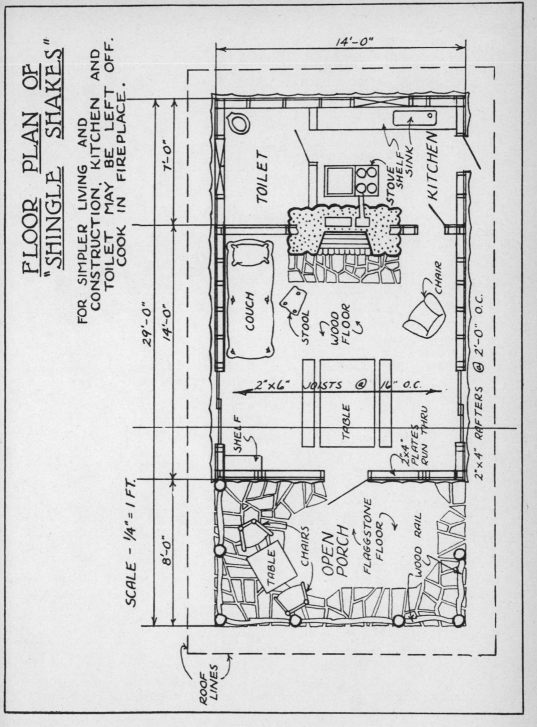

FLOOR PLAN OF "SHINGLE SHAKES"

FOR SIMPLER LIVING AND CONSTRUCTION, KITCHEN AND TOILET MAY BE LEFT OFF. COOK IN FIREPLACE.

SCALE - ¼" = 1 FT.

14'-0"

29'-0"

7'-0"

14'-0"

8'-0"

TOILET

KITCHEN

STOVE

SHELF

SINK

CHAIR

COUCH

STOOL

WOOD FLOOR

TABLE

2"x6" JOISTS @ 16" O.C.

2"x4" RAFTERS @ 2'-0" O.C.

SHELF

2"x4" PLATES RUN THRU

CHAIRS

TABLE

OPEN PORCH

FLAGSTONE FLOOR

WOOD RAIL

ROOF LINES

LONG HOUSE

THE MAIN BUILDING, 14'x36', IS BUILT OF LOGS AND DIVIDED INTO THREE ROOMS — KITCHEN AND TOILET ARE FRAME AND SHINGLED — USE FLAGGSTONE FLOOR THROUGHOUT — STOVE IN CENTER ROOM REFLECTS THE HEAT OF EACH FIREPLACE AND KITCHEN STOVE HEATS TOILET AND KITCHEN.

2"x6" RAFTERS

TOP OF RIDGE POLE

4'-2"

TOP OF PLATE

7'-0"

7'-0"

DOOR

FLAGG STONE FL. PITCH TO WEATHER · CONCRETE

KITCHEN AND BATH

SECTION THRU PORCH | SECTION THRU BEDROOM

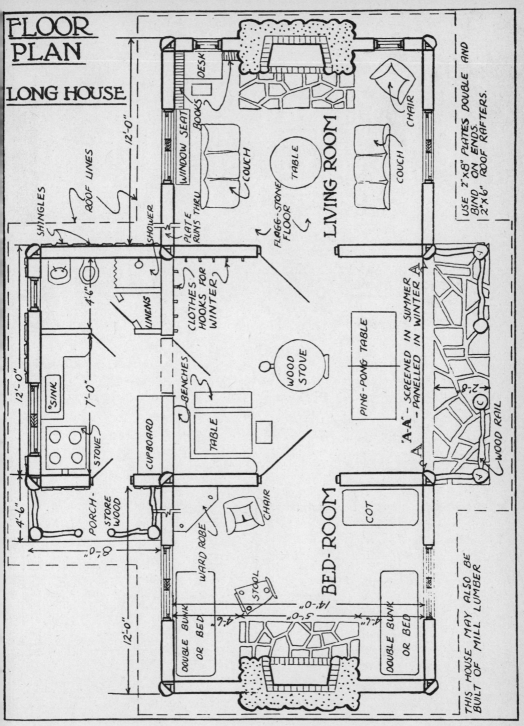

FLOOR PLAN
LONG HOUSE

SHINGLES

ROOF LINES

WINDOW SEAT

BOOKS

DESK

COUCH

CHAIR

COUCH

TABLE

FLAGG-STONE FLOOR

LIVING ROOM

USE 2"x8" PLATES DOUBLE AND BIND ON ENDS. 2"x6" ROOF RAFTERS.

12'-0"

SHOWER

PLATE RUNS THRU

LINENS

CLOTHES HOOKS FOR WINTER

4'-6"

12'-0"

SINK

STOVE

7'-0"

CUPBOARD

BENCHES

TABLE

WOOD STOVE

PING-PONG TABLE

"A-A" - SCREENED IN SUMMER PANELLED IN WINTER

WOOD RAIL

2'-0"

PORCH-

STORE WOOD

4'-6"

8'-0"

WARD ROBE

CHAIR

BED-ROOM

COT

DOUBLE BUNK OR BED

STOOL

DOUBLE BUNK OR BED

12'-0"

14'-0"

4'-6"

5'-0"

4'-6"

THIS HOUSE MAY ALSO BE BUILT OF MILL LUMBER

37

"THE SQUATTER"

BUILT IN ONE DAY BY TWO MEN. HEATS QUICKLY —NO UNDER DRAUGHTS.

SHEET IRON STOVE MAY BE SUBSTITUTED FOR FIREPLACE.

WITH HEAVY SNOW IT WILL KEEP WARM IN SUB-ZERO WEATHER USE 2x4 TIMBERS THROUGHOUT. USE THIS CABIN BEFORE YOU BUILD YOUR PRIZE CABIN.

KITCHEN SHELF

TABLE

CHEST

BUNK

BUNK

STORAGE

STORAGE

12'-0"

Let's Go
to Work

Let's Go to Work

WHEN you really get serious about building a Cabin-in-the-Woods you will very quickly envision rather definite ideas of your own. By all means hold on to them. The ideas are usually larger and surrounded with more grandeur, more spacious quarters, added acres often beyond your finances to carry them through. Then comes the paring down process to fit the pocketbook. At this point you may welcome suggestions, but you do not want to be told, "This is the only way," or "This is the only kind of a cabin." After all this is your project. It will mean little when finished unless it has your personality, your own innovations, your own architecture built into the sum total. Perhaps these offerings may stimulate your thinking and planning. They may save you some of the errors commonly made. Lengthy descriptions have purposely been avoided. There is no one way. Your own aptitude, your own peculiar kind of initiative and the ability to use your hands, together with native intelligence (horse sense) precludes any one from trespassing with the final answer. So if I can be your helper, let's go to work.

Your "treasure chest" is really your tool chest full of sharp tools. You can save yourself endless trouble and add to your enjoyment by building a tool box for your tools. It is your "treasure chest;" for these, plus your own "wildest" ideas and your own will to express yourself, will lift you into the realm of the genius—the creator making dreams come true.

It will speed up your work if the chest is arranged with a place for each tool. They will keep sharp longer. But most of all, you will not have to buy new ones to replace those lost. The chest, too, will serve as a table for those campfire meals while your cabin is in the making. An added cushion will make it a part of your cabin furniture.

Only simple tools are needed. Keep them sharp. Respect them.

Cross-cut hand saw
Rip saw
Key-hole saw
Claw hammer
Level
Plumb line
Three-quarter length axe
Hand axe
One-quarter-inch chisel
One inch chisel
Wrecking bar
Square
Shovel
Crow-bar
Pick

File
Mason's trowel
Mason's narrow trowel
Putty knife
Tin snips
Cross-cut saw for logs
Jack plane
Draw shave
Chalk line
Carborundum stone
Two three-inch paint brushes
Carpenter's twine
Six-foot rule
A cant hook will help in handling large logs

BUILDING RULES YOU MAY NOT VIOLATE

Anyone with a general working knowledge of tools can build his own cabin, if he follows a few simple, but fundamental rules:

(1) Set foundation or piers below frost line. If in deep woods, freezing is not as severe. Bank your cabin in the fall with leaves.

(2) Set foundation both level and truly square. This will save endless trouble as building develops. Triangle of three, four and five feet will give you a large square; also six, eight and ten feet. Here is how you do it. Drive a stake (A) firmly into the ground at the corner of your planned cabin. Mark a cross (X) on the top. From the center of this cross measure off exactly three feet along the side of your cabin and then drive the second stake (B). At right angles to this line and starting again from the first stake (A), measure off four feet and drive a stake (C). This done, measure from (B) to (C). It must measure exactly five feet and you then have a right angle triangle with (A) at the base. If it does not measure exactly five feet, move stake (C) until it does. Your whole structure will reveal good lines by the care you exercise in the use of the Plane, Plumb line, or Level and the Square.

(3) Square, level and plumb tell the truth. Never guess.

(4) Sharp tools will speed up the work.

(5) Provide for thorough drainage about cabin.

(6) Build from a plan, not memory. Don't rush it through in a week-end. Take a month, six months or a year. Your greatest pleasure will be in the building and your greatest enjoyment will be in the satisfaction of a comfortable, snug and well built cabin.

(7) If in doubt seek expert advice.

LAND COST

Land can be secured at surprisingly low cost or at low rental. Poor farm land, i.e. land cut deep with ravines, is of little value to the farmer and ideal for our purpose, especially if there are trees, bushes, shrubs.

Over the past thirty years I have traveled the length and breadth of this country. Whether New York State, Florida, the Rockies or the Prairie lands of the southwest, there is an unlimited quantity of land available. More than this, it can be purchased as low as one dollar per acre.

The trouble with most of us is that we want so many feet frontage on a lake or stream or ocean. Or we want the highest hill for view. For these, of course, we must pay. Let us think simply. A bit of land, say five acres, off the main highway, a lovely view to the south, a real vista after removing one or two trees and bushes. The land is rough and rocky, but this is no obstacle. It's a challenge, for here we shall build a rock gardens, trails, out-of-door rustic stove for picnic suppers.

You will find plenty of land for your purpose "off the beaten path," and it will be within your means. If you do not wish to own the land, you can work out a rental arrangement say for five, ten or fifteen years.

If you live in a big city, the distance to travel will be greater. Do not cast the idea of a Cabin-in-the-Woods aside just because you may not own an automobile. It still can be done even if you have to take the bus or trolley or train. It will help you to grow strong and more resourceful. Yes—it will increase your earning power. Some day you may have that auto, also a trailer.

CABIN COST

That all depends on how lavish you wish to be and based on your own resources—how many rooms, how much land. A snug cabin may be built for as low as fifty dollars and up to four, six hundred or to several thousand dollars. Remember, the purpose of this book is to help the novice who wants to play a big part in building his own cabin; who wants to be resourceful.

If to hire your labor instead of doing most of it yourself, if to buy rustic furniture instead of creating it out of woods material, if to be in a hurry to complete your Cabin-in-the-Woods— then, of course, costs will mount. A good slogan to keep in mind is, "Utilize all natural resources. Do it yourself. Take time." Even hinges, doorlocks, coat hangers, shelves, shingles, stone steps and slab floors need nothing more than a few tools, the natural resources at your disposal and the will to make it your own handicraft.

If this is your first cabin building experience, avoid larger cabins than here suggested, for both carpentering and structural problems will present themselves that are not included in these plates. A big cabin needs additional reinforcing, heavier timber, supports, et cetera. You will become discouraged. Our forefathers, the old pioneers, built small cabins and lived in them. You will lose the lore and spirit of a Cabin-in-the-Woods with a big house. Again, a good carpenter is not necessarily a good log cabin builder. Different technique is involved and you gain this technique through experience. You will later want to build another and will benefit by your first experience.

LOGS FOR YOUR CABIN

Choose soft woods rather than hard woods for your first experience—hemlock, bass, pine—even poplar works up easily into logs. By all means avoid working with oak logs unless you are thoroughly familiar with this wood. It is "temperamental." I have seen it after it was thoroughly dried, seasoned, squared and fitted into place, change form a year after the cabin was built. It will twist slightly like a barber pole even to lifting your cabin at one corner and leaving big cracks to patch from year to year. But that's another story.

Speaking of green soft-wood logs—it will pay you to remove the bark. Use a draw-shave. Insects get under the bark and may cause you much annoyance. There are methods of preserving the bark, but I still favor stripping the logs. It will give you a clean cabin. Old cedar telephone poles redressed are recommended, if you can get them. They are dry and ready for use. Dressing old telephone poles is fun, and will give most satisfying results. The grain in cedar logs is straight. With a sharp axe, dig in about one inch all around. The wood will come off in long strips—two, three and four feet long. After the rough axe work, finish and smooth off with a draw-shave. Your logs will look like new timber and the sweet smell of cedar will reward you for your added effort.

Fourteen logs with an average thickness of eight or nine inches and twenty-six feet long will build a cabin twelve by fourteen feet up to fourteen by sixteen feet; depending upon the number of doors and windows.

Pile the logs far enough apart and crisscross so as to give them all the air possible for drying. If the logs are green it is best to allow them to dry several months before using. When hauling your logs to your cabin site, place them equally on either side of the planned building. This will save unnecessary loads after the logs are sawed up. Remove knots and burls so as to have logs as nearly straight and smooth as possible.

TIE YOUR CABIN TOGETHER

There are three important places to bind your cabin:

(1) After placing the sill logs, which rest on the foundation and should, of course, run parallel to each other, place your floor joist running at right angles to the sills. The log sills should be dug out to accommodate the two inch by six inch floor joists and then nailed in securely. This binds your floor both ways after you lay a double floor.

(2) The next place to tie-in is at the plates which rest on top of your logs and corner studs

and form the base for your roof construction to fasten to. Plates should be two inch by six inch laid double and over-lapped at every corner, so as to bind and leave no weak spots. Logs may be used as plates and they, too, should overlap at corners and then be bolted together as well as spiked to corner studs.

(3) The third important tie-in is in the roof rafters, for a hip roof will spread, especially under heavy snows and so roof rafters should be bound together to hold your roof rigid. In northern zones where there is a great deal of snow, more rafters should be added. The floor joists should be of two inch by six inch lumber supported in the middle, and the roof rafters for the size cabin here suggested can be of two inch by six inch, but preferably of saplings dressed and trimmed—all about four or five inches in diameter.

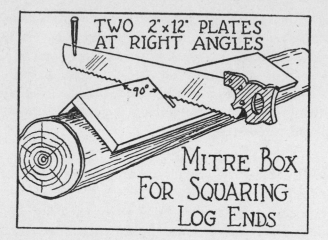

TWO 2"x12" PLATES AT RIGHT ANGLES

90°

MITRE BOX FOR SQUARING LOG ENDS

MAINE WOODS METHOD OF BINDING LOGS AT CORNERS

The old-fashioned method of notching logs is more costly and requires the skill of a woodsman. It requires at least four additional feet on each log and unless expertly done will be a disappointment to you. If you are familiar with axemanship and have the time, then by all means notch your logs.

The Maine Woods Method saves time, labor and material, and gives you very satisfactory results. After the foundation logs or sills have been placed and squared, toe-nail a double or "V" studding at each corner—that is a two inch by six inch stud spiked at right angles to a two inch by eight inch, so that the two are "V" shaped. (Use six penny spikes.) The outside will measure eight inches; the inside six inches. Place this on the sill at the corner so that the mouth of the "V" faces outside. (At bay window intersections, the mouth of the "V" faces inside.)

A "V" studding now placed at every corner of the cabin and carefully toe-nailed, should be topped with a double plate or two two inch by eight inch running all around or a log or overlapping. Be sure the two inch by eight inch plates bind or over-lap at all points.

Cut logs with care to fit exactly between your "V" studding or doorjamb and windows, then spike with six penny spikes through the stud wall and into the end of the log. Use at least three spikes for each end of log. Pack spaces between end of log and studding with oakum. Keep logs spaced at least one inch apart to provide for generous chinking.

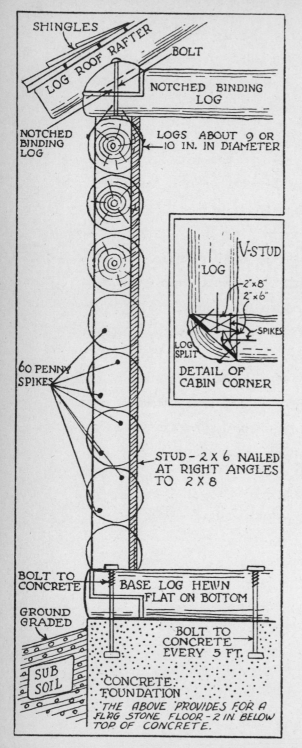

Labels within figure:

SHINGLES

LOG ROOF RAFTER

BOLT

NOTCHED BINDING LOG

NOTCHED BINDING LOG

LOGS ABOUT 9 OR 10 IN. IN DIAMETER

V-STUD

LOG

2" x 8"
2" x 6"

SPIKES

LOG SPLIT

DETAIL OF CABIN CORNER

60 PENNY SPIKES

STUD - 2 X 6 NAILED AT RIGHT ANGLES TO 2 X 8

BOLT TO CONCRETE

BASE LOG HEWN FLAT ON BOTTOM

GROUND GRADED

BOLT TO CONCRETE EVERY 5 FT.

SUB SOIL

CONCRETE FOUNDATION

THE ABOVE PROVIDES FOR A FLAG STONE FLOOR - 2 IN. BELOW TOP OF CONCRETE.

CABIN DETAIL

Here is a complete picture story of the Maine Woods cabin construction from the foundation to roof rafters.

Concrete foundation down below the frost line; base logs anchored by bolts to the foundation.

Next we have "V" studs at all corners with logs spiked at ends; log plates properly notched, bolted and anchored; finally roof log rafters to complete the log frame.

The insert presents in detail the "V" stud construction.

Study these plates until you are thoroughly familiar with every detail. Build your miniature from these plates. This type of log cabin construction is really very economical as against overlapping logs. It will give you a sturdy building "tight as a drum."

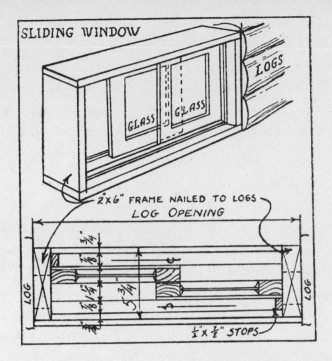

SLIDING WINDOW

LOGS

GLASS   GLASS

2"x6" FRAME NAILED TO LOGS

LOG OPENING

LOG   LOG

½"x⅞" STOPS

WINDOWS, DOORS AND GABLES

According to the thickness of your logs, build your own window frames out of two inch by six inch or two inch by eight inch lumber and place windows in double, so that they overlap and slide past each other. Place strips on the outside and inside of the window, so that they may slide back and forth. This removes hinges and the inconvenience of having windows inside of a room when they are open. As you bring your logs up to the desired height, place your whole window frame on the log and build a-round it. Be sure your frame is exactly squared. Do this by keeping it braced both ways on

51

the frame. You can purchase from your wood-mill dealer almost any size windows you wish. Your cabin is likely to be dark unless you provide one window large enough to give ample light. There is no need for feeling cooped up. It costs a little more, but it is worth it.

Be sure to put a small opening in the gables of your Cabin-in-the-Woods—both ends. These for ventilators. You can control these by a shutter-string. Screen them on the outside. Leave them slightly open when you leave your cabin and you will find it sweet and fresh smelling when you return. On the coldest night you can sleep comfortably with plenty of fresh air by opening these two vents and also by the dead air that will be drawn out by your fireplace.

Build your door-frames out of two inch by six inch or two inch by eight inch lumber and place strips inside the door-jamb against which to fit the door. The door-jamb serves also as a stud. Nail through it to hold your log.

DRAINAGE AND GRADING

Certainly you should not choose a marshy spot for your cabin. It is self evident there would be dampness, wet floors, rheumatism, the doctor.

Choose first a knoll or high ground that pitches down from your cabin site. Rain, but especially melting snow, will flow away from your cabin. This is a rule you may not change if you want a dry cabin.

Of course you want your cabin to nestle into its surroundings. Give it, however, at least eighteen inches elevation above the natural ground and have it drain down and away from your building on all sides. The ground dug out from the foundation, or should you decide to dig a cellar, should be thrown outside the foundation. You won't have to dig the foundation so deep if you raise the level without.

To do a really fine job, especially if you use a flagstone floor within, is to lay a three-inch tile at bottom of foundation on the outside. Be sure it pitches downward from one side of the building all around to the point where it drains down the hillside.

UPPER AND LOWER BUNKS CONVERTED INTO COUCH

By building in upper and lower bunks, upper bunk can be hinged. Drop front of upper bunk to form back rest of couch with lower bunk.

PAINTING AND PRESERVATIVES

As you read more into this subject you will find many recommendations. The old pioneer had no paint or stain and his building stood the test of time. Window frames, window sills, door-jambs and doors can be painted, or better, stained.

Beautiful effects can be had by working out a weather-stain color. After your logs have thoroughly dried, it will be a far better time to stain with preservatives.

CHINKING

Chinking between logs will make a cabin warm, clean and dry. It should be carefully done. It pays in the end. Logs must be dried thoroughly. Plaster with sand four parts, lime one-half to one part, white cement one part. If spaces of one inch or more occur between logs, fill in with small branches nailed to top and bottom logs, inside and out. Don't be too sparing with plaster. Wide plaster spaces will brighten the room, too. Plaster well if you want a warm cabin. The plaster on the outside should not touch or meet the plaster on the inside for the dead-air space makes the best non-conductor. To make plaster hold between logs, drive nails as far in as possible into logs both up and down near middle of crack—many of them—say every three or four inches—old nails, crooked nails. Another good method is to nail in woven wire or hardware cloth, one-quarter inch mesh. Cut the hardware cloth in strips about three inches wide; fold lengthwise in a slight "V" shape and drive in between logs and nail to upper or lower log. This is not absolutely neces-

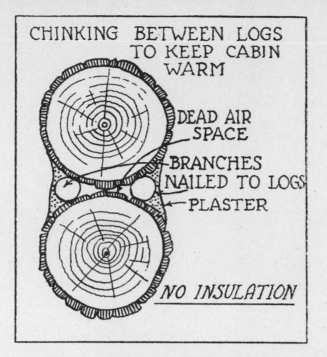

CHINKING BETWEEN LOGS
TO KEEP CABIN
WARM

DEAD AIR
SPACE

BRANCHES
NAILED TO LOGS

PLASTER

NO INSULATION

sary, but gives added strength. Dead-air space makes perfect non-conductor.

Better to chink with moss if logs are not thoroughly dry or leave unchinked until dry. Lime one part, sand three parts, wood-ashes twenty-five parts, salt two parts, thoroughly mixed with dry moss will serve well for a hunter's lodge. The ashes tend to keep vermin away.

When chinking is complete, if any light spots show through a door or windowjambs, caulk with tarred hemp or oakum, or moss. The tar smell soon disappears. Be especially careful to chink between ground or sill log above before laying floor.

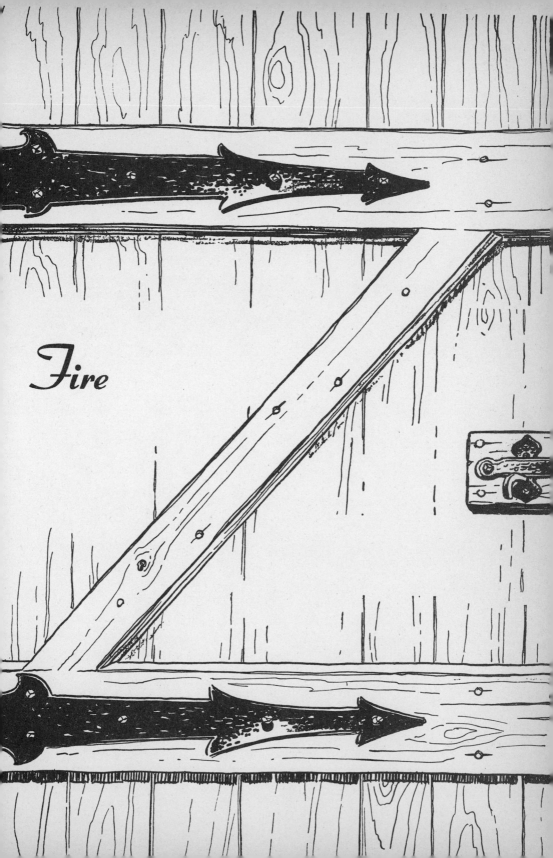

Fire

"The Sacrament of Fire"

Kneel always when you light a fire!
Kneel reverently, and thankful be
For God's unfailing charity,
And on the ascending flame inspire
A little prayer, which shall upbear
The incense of your thankfulness
For this sweet grace
Of warmth and light!
For here again is sacrifice
For your delight.

Oak, elm and chestnut, beech and red pine bole.
God shrined His sunshine, and enwombed
For you these stores of light and heat,
Your life-joys to complete.
These all have died that you might live:
Yours now the high prerogative
To loose their long captivitie's,
And through these new activities
A wider life to give.
Kneel always when you light a fire.
Kneel reverently,
And grateful be
For God's unfailing charity.

John Oxenham.

(By gracious permission of his
daughter Erica Oxenham)

Fireplaces

SUCCESSFULLY BUILT BY THE NOVICE

WORKING with brick and mortar is fascinating. It will give you thorough respect for this craft. Fireplace building is hard work, back breaking, yet worth all the effort in the pleasure a glowing hearth will give. Diligent application and any handyman with a few tools and the will to "stick" can succeed. Our forefathers had to rely on their own skill or develop it. It's just a part of the American spirit.

First of all, let us make it attractive—simple lines, stones from the field, fit them together like patterns in a flagstone floor. Flat sand- or limestones work up best. Fashioning stones from the field for your fireplace will present some problems and an occasional "frustration." With a little practice and perseverance, however, you will suddenly discover you can split a stone with precision. You will experience a new thrill. This, then, is learning by doing and in the doing you will find yourself tired, muscles a bit sore, hands hardened and rough, but you will say over and over again, "I did it. I have it. I know it." You will go to bed wholesomely tired, but eager to get off to an early start in the morning, to work again on your fireplace.

Use natural material if available, before resorting to brick. Be sure, however, to line your fireplace with fire brick.

Do not attempt a large fireplace if it is your first experiment. The two fireplaces shown are workable. One is different, raised fourteen inches above the floor, with shelf which makes excellent space for cooking and will save your back. It warms the body and the room—not just the shins.

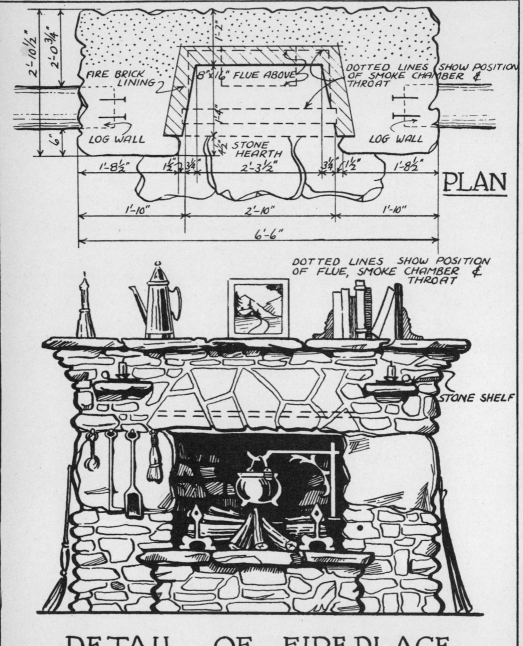

PLAN

DETAIL OF FIREPLACE
WITH RAISED HEARTH

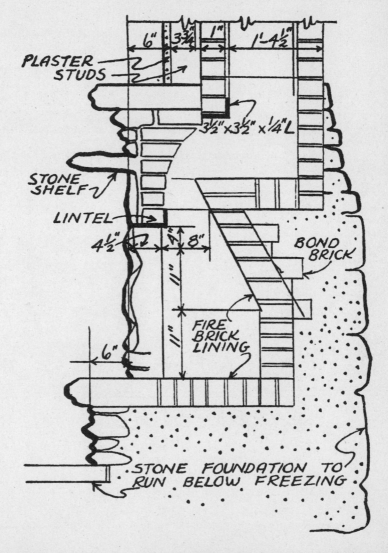

PLASTER
STUDS

6" 3½" 1" 1'-4½"

3½"×3½"×¼"L

STONE
SHELF

LINTEL

4½" 4" 8"

BOND
BRICK

11"

11"

FIRE
BRICK
LINING

6"

STONE FOUNDATION TO
RUN BELOW FREEZING

CROSS-SECTION OF RAISED HEARTH FIREPLACE

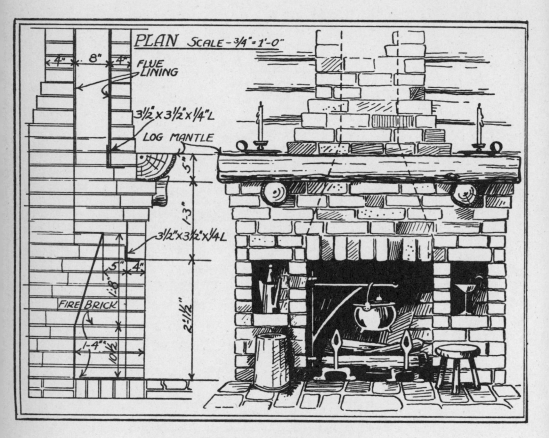

SMALL BRICK FIREPLACE

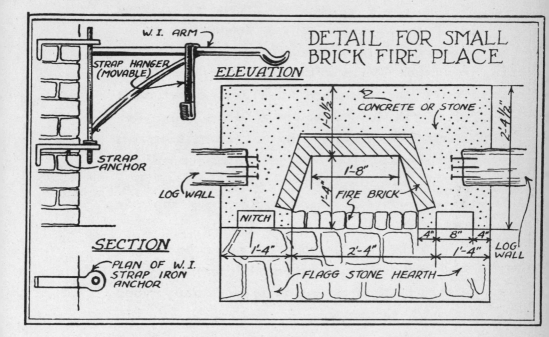

DETAIL FOR SMALL BRICK FIRE PLACE

W. I. ARM

STRAP HANGER (MOVABLE)

ELEVATION

CONCRETE OR STONE

STRAP ANCHOR

LOG WALL

FIRE BRICK

1'-8"

1'-4"

NITCH

SECTION

PLAN OF W.I. STRAP IRON ANCHOR

1'-4"

2'-4"

4" 8" 4"

1'-4"

FLAGG STONE HEARTH

LOG WALL

IMPORTANT

Build your fireplace in end of room away from doors, to give snugness and avoid drafts. Your fireplace will give warmth, a welcome glow and throw shadows. Do not expect a fireplace to keep a cabin warm in sub-zero weather. Place a wood burning stove at opposite ends of room. Run smoke-stack through roof with metal collar. You will then be between two fires and warmed both "fore and aft."

THE "WHY" OF FIREPLACES
THAT BURN WELL

It is really tragic to see so many lovely cabins spoiled by smoking fireplaces. A good many fireplaces are built by people who do not understand the first principles of fireplace construction. Books on the subject are available at your library, also the United States Department of Agriculture Farmers Bulletin No. 1649 treats this subject at length. If measurements here given are followed, your fireplace will not smoke, but will burn perfectly, keeping logs burning overnight and will be a joy in your cabin.

After your fireplace has dried out for a few days, light your first really great fire. What a thrill! It works. Call in the family, your friends. Celebrate.

If it smokes, sit alone and study it. Watch the air currents. Light a fagot and hold it at the upper corners of the opening. If the flue does not draw the flame and smoke, then there is something wrong about the throat. Get your chisel and dig inside on either side of the throat above the lintel. Here is the greatest possibility of trouble. If you are sure the flue is in correct measured relationship to the opening, you really can't go very wrong. After you have adjusted here and there until the fireplace really burns, you will approach the next fireplace with added confidence and will have good results.

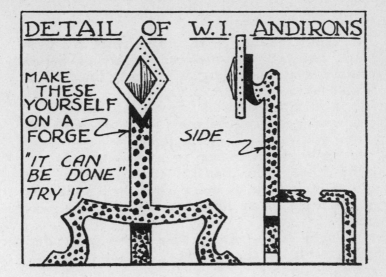

TOOLS

Level, plumb line, mixing box two by four feet and ten inches deep, hoe, trowel, mason's hammer, chalk line, square, shovel.

MATERIALS

Stones or bricks, sand, gravel, cement, lime, nails, chalk, iron lintel arch support, eight inches longer than width of opening (angle iron lintel will not sag), one hundred fire brick, twenty-five pounds of fire clay, pothooks, pothook supports.

HOW TO PROCEED

Build foundation the full size of the fireplace, two feet to four-feet-six inches below ground level, according to freezing line; fill in with concrete and stones.

Rest floor joists on fireplace foundation. Fill in with concrete between joists to floor level, unless you plan a flagstone floor.

Build the fireplace by levels—i.e., do not build up one side, then the other. If you add a four-inch stone on one corner, bring the rest of the fireplace up likewise, then add the next tier.

Make it rough. If one stone protrudes, good, but bring the one above it back true with your plumb line.

Rake out the mortar about one inch deep between joists. This will give an aged or weathered appearance. Keep your mortar stiff, i.e., not too much water.

A false hearth is cheaper, but not so sturdy. Build hearth the full width of the fireplace.

If a log cabin, the fireplace foundation must be deeper front to back to allow for thickness of logs.

Bring foundation to within six inches of floor and make level. Now lay your fireplace out carefully, providing space for fire-brick and keeping in mind support for chimney which must rest on foundation outside of cabin. Use your plumb line.

Do not be sparing with mortar. Mortar must be free from gravel, not too wet. Use sifted sand mixed to a stiff paste. Place face stones about three-quarters of an inch apart; fill in between joints. Tap stones with handle of trowel until all joints are well cemented. Scrape off surplus and throw back into mortar box. Mix mortar in small quantities and work it with trowel from time to time to keep it tempered. Total of three to five shovelfuls.

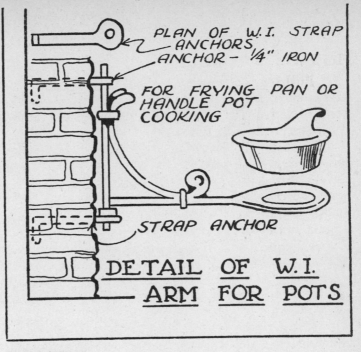

PLAN OF W.I. STRAP ANCHORS
ANCHOR — ¼" IRON

FOR FRYING PAN OR HANDLE POT COOKING

STRAP ANCHOR

DETAIL OF W.I. ARM FOR POTS

MIXTURE

Three sand, one cement, one and one-half lime or prepared commercial mixture called "Brick Cement"—directions on the bag.

It is advisable to build the chimney of brick, enclosing flue. Use flue lining eight inches by twelve inches for fireplace with an opening of thirty-six inches by twenty-four inches. Lay the firebrick first and then build the stone work around it. This keeps the work open and easy to get at.

The inside of the raised hearth fireplace measures thirty-six inches wide, twenty to twenty-four inches in depth and twenty-six inches high. The sides draw in slightly toward the back (about two inches each side). The back wall rises perpendicular for fourteen inches from fireplace level, then slants upward and forward until it reaches the throat which is at least eight inches above the arch. The throat should be at least ten per cent in square area of the opening of the fireplace. Also the flue must be ten per cent in square area of the opening of the fireplace or better.

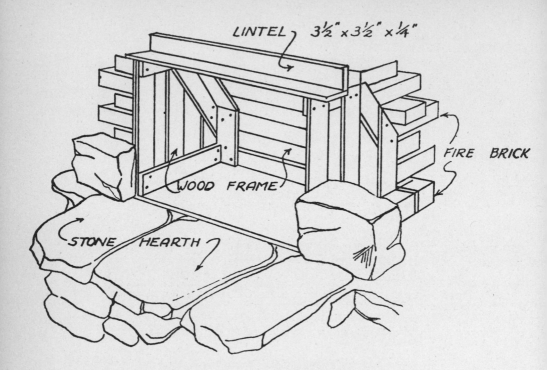

LINTEL — 3½" x 3½" x ¼"

FIRE BRICK

WOOD FRAME

STONE HEARTH

A SIMPLE METHOD FOR THE NOVICE

First build a wooden box or frame, the outside of which will be the same as the inside space of your fireplace—throat and approach to the flue. This will save you endless trouble. Build your fireplace and mason work around the frame work with reasonable certainty. Always lay brick or stone horizontal and bind one on the other. Use care in placing damper and the two angle irons. Damper is not necessary, but will save your house from destruction by squirrels in the summer and fall; also helps regulate draft. An old-fashioned damper such as used in wood stove pipe can be built out of sheet iron and fitted in flue just above fireplace mantle shelf. The rest then is a matter of laying one stone or brick on the other always lapping one stone over the other, keeping all work level and perpendicular lines true.

POT HOOKS

When building your fireplace do not forget to include an iron hook on which to hang a kettle for hot water. A swinging pothook has many valuable uses—keeping food hot, keeping coffee hot, et cetera.

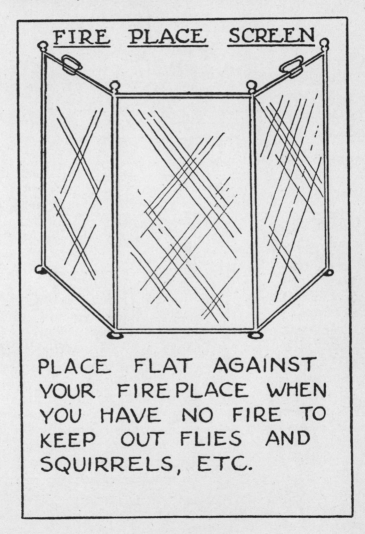

FIRE PLACE SCREEN

PLACE FLAT AGAINST YOUR FIREPLACE WHEN YOU HAVE NO FIRE TO KEEP OUT FLIES AND SQUIRRELS, ETC.

FIRE PLACE TOOLS

COOKING GRAT

2' 10"

5"

BUILD OF ¾" ANGLE IRON-
PLACE NEAR FRONT OF
HEARTH AND DRAW HO
COALS UNDER
GRATE.

TOASTER - FOR
STEAKS, CHOPS,
ETC.

Ashes

It's time to turn in, for the hour is late. The night is still. Yet somehow we linger. Why? No one knows. There is always enchantment in the closing hour when the fading coals in the fire stir and "speak" their soft good night. Dying embers fall apart; the glow fades and is replaced by a delicate white ash, more beautiful and as intriguing as the stillness of the night. Finally we realize the great sacrament of fire is completed. A down-draft of our chimney may scatter these feathery white ashes over our hearth until one becomes entranced by the lacy white filament. "Ashes to ashes" have portrayed their fulfillment.

Somehow I just can't bear to burn rubbish or wastepaper in a glowing fireplace. These produce a black ash. White ashes remind one of the "Sacrament of Fire," of God's gift, of warmth and light. The delicate loveliness of white wood ashes seems a symbol of purity and consecration. We, too, will "burn out" some day, but joyously by what we have created in our time for our own happiness and the good of the world. We, too, may contribute to life's great "sacrament of fire" for the generations to come.

"Tell me what you eat and I will tell you what you are"—Anthelme Brillat-Savarin

"Cooking is become an art, a noble science; cooks are gentlemen"—Robert Burton

OUTDOOR COOKING

Build your "wildest" notion of an outdoor fireplace. You don't have to follow conventional lines. There are none. The above sketch offers a suggestion. In this drawing there is place for your firewood to keep dry, shelves, the grate warming plate, a chimney high enough to pass smoke above your head. In the center and below is the bake oven, closed by a flat stone or iron sheet. It has a separate flue. Build a good fire in it. Get it hot. Rake out the coals and ashes. Throw an ash-wood shaving four inches long inside. If it curls up, the ends touching, you have better than four hundred degrees temperature. (Tuck away under the eaves of your cabin a piece of ashwood for this temperature finding purpose.) That's how our pioneer mothers did it. Bake Boston Beans, plank fish, wild-apple pie, coffee-cake or actually salt-rising bread.

Make the outdoor stove in your yard a place where your friends will gather. Place benches and garden chairs around it. They will re-discover that cooking is not drudgery, but an art of creating delectables. Here is the place to create new dishes according to your own ideas. Try cooking with olive oil—you'll like it. Try okra, egg plant, try out different spices. Your friends will be attracted. Recipes and new dishes will be shared.

What makes an out-of-doors meal is first of all the out-of-doors. The very setting is important. Floating clouds, the call of wildlife, birds overhead—the smell of pungent pines wafted past you and through you. Have you ever waked up refreshed after a good night's sleep out in the open and eaten sour-dough pancakes as only an old prospector in the Rockies can bake them? Let's have breakfast with one of these old "sour-doughs." The delicate sizzling noise of frying bacon, sputtering eggs, the rich aroma of coffee simmering in its blackened coffee pot. It does something to you. An occasional whiff of smoke from the campfire and a stack of golden brown sour-dough cakes. I still thrill to that morning years ago when camping on Cripple Creek, Colorado, Harry E. Moreland, that grand old camper-prospector yelled, "The burnt offering is now served!"

To prepare such a meal over the campfire, with a nicety, without smearing pot-black over one's face and clothes, will add to the art of living happily in the out-of-doors.

OUTDOOR COOKERY IN THE GARDEN FIREPLACE

Cooking in your garden fireplace is not only fun, it's getting back to nature. It is a real art. For perfect family companionship and participation there is nothing in this world that will give you and yours more satisfaction, the sense of accomplishment, and satisfaction after it is done with, than a family-cooked royal meal prepared in your outdoor garden fireplace.

If you want your friends to come often, try the out-of-door cooking party. They won't come just to eat. You will have created a new and intriguing situation. Your friends will say, "When do we have another? We'll bring the steaks—we'll bring anything you say, but let's have another garden dinner party."

Outdoor cooking is indeed an art in itself. While women do most of the cooking and preparing of meals within the home, the outdoor cooking is, to my thinking, the man's job. I say a man's job partly to reciprocate—perhaps a bit boastfully—to show that he, too, can "do his stuff," but most of all to satisfy that low-down ornery quality of man's ego—to prove he can prepare a meal worthy of the name. So, Sir, enjoy the plaudits of your guests, accept the passing approval of your wife and daughters, revel when the meal is over in the wholesale enthusiastic approbation of, "What a cook!"

To accomplish all this, there are a few techniques to be observed. Can you build the fire, cook the meal and serve it while dressed in white duck trousers and sport shirt and come through clean and spotless? I'm now talking to the men-folks. To do this is an art and a very dainty one. Remember, unless you do "your stuff," your wife will laugh at you and you will decide better to stay in your own field, whatever your calling.

A few simple suggestions before you start your meal and before you put on your white trapping:

(1) Take with you to your cooking "den" all needed equipment.

(2) Have sufficient wood for the fire (three armsfull or more).

(3) Be sure to include a good axe and a low box or table with cover.

(4) Be sure your fire burns long enough to build up a good bed of coals. Replenish your fire three times with hard wood if you want hot coals and really hot coals are the secret of a successfully cooked outdoor meal. Please don't make the common error of cooking over flames. They only blacken your pots, give unsteady heat—first burning your food and often leaving it half-cooked, underdone—faugh!

(5) Take with you a towel and if you can, a basin of water and soap. This will

HOW DO YOU LIKE YOUR STEAK?

Rare
Medium
Well Done
Roasted

help make you a clean outdoor cook and keep your duck trousers white throughout.

(6) Include a few old newspapers; especially if you must put your steak grill on the grass, as well as kettles of vegetables and other foodstuffs. When through, burn the paper and destroy any evidence of untidyness.

(7) Be sure to bring the salt and pepper shakers, a long fork and necessary utensils for your meal. You will spoil the dignity of your attempted culinary art if you have to run back to the kitchen for this or that. "What will mother say!"

Now let's have a one-inch steak for our party tonight. This calls for a bit of argument with the meat man. You prefer tenderloin, T-bone, sirloin? You want it so thick? How long has it been cured? Soon he will meet your requirements. It finds its way into your ice box until the appointed hour. In all my experience of broiling steaks to make them just really perfect when served, calls for one sure approach. No matter how badly you cook your steak, no matter how much it is overdone or underdone, you won't go far wrong at any time if you are sure your meat man gave you really good steaks. If it comes out right and the steak is delicious, take full credit for it. Chances are you won't deserve the credit, until you have learned to select a good steak.

Broiling steak is as old as time; yet too many steaks could be better if a few simple precautions were taken. I prefer a one-inch steak. Thicker steaks, say two inches, are hard to broil in an outdoor fireplace unless you have had long experience.

When we talk of rare steak, do we mean red inside? Dripping in blood? Not for me. The rare steak, to my taste, should have had the effect of the coals heating it to a thorough hot throughout. If you like your steak raw, better serve it raw and call it a "cannibal" steak.

Place your steaks in a toaster grill. Put one-half inch strips of bacon across the steak at three-inch intervals and at right angles to the wire of your grill. Bacon enriches the flavor. Place the grill on your bed of hot coals. (Put a half-brick at far side of your coals and a fresh green log nearest you on which to rest the grill.) The grill should be about two inches from the coals. Let it sizzle for two minutes.

Then turn over. This done, turn back again. Listen to the grease drip into the hot coals. Watch it jump into the flames. Good! Let it burn. Let the flames play around the steaks for about three minutes *wildly!* Turn the grill over and repeat. If flames do not start at once, throw in a shaving. (Have you a jackknife? It counts in broiling a good steak.) After three more minutes of "wild" burning of your steak, you will have a perfect one—burnt brown on the outside, juicy and rare within. For your guests who want well-done steaks, just roast them a bit longer. Salt and pepper and butter before serving.

The meal over with, you will soon start singing folk-songs, chatting, singing again. Someone brings a guitar or banjo. Soon there are blinking stars. Again a lovely night. In season we find lovely, inspiring nights in any part of this global world. Let's use them. Call in your guests, your friends, for a supper about your outdoor garden fireplace.

"THE HOT-DOG, BACON AND MELTED CHEESE DREAM"

For a simple picnic meal at little cost, but big returns, try a "Hot-Dog, Bacon and Melted Cheese Dream." Wieners or "hot dogs," one or more for each member in the party, split in half lengthwise. Place within a a thin slice of American cheese. Now slit a strip of bacon lengthwise and roll the half piece around the wiener like a barber pole. Place in a reflector oven before fire and roast. After a few minutes of broiling, turn wieners around to roast on other side. After another eight minutes your meat and cheese "dreams" are ready—cheese melted and oozing out. Have the buns or bread toasted and hot. Pot of coffee or tea, and here you have a tasty picnic meal. Add radishes, celery, olives. (Helps in the roughage.) Now a bit of fruit or the added home-made pie prepared by mother. Yum, yum.

Burn up the paper plates and cups and go home with no worry about dish washing. Reflect on a perfect day and you haven't ruined your pocketbook. Every meal need not be a banquet. The fun of eating includes companionship, working together, the sparkle of the fireplace, cooling embers and confidences.

CHEESE AND CRACKERS

Brown the crackers in the fireplace reflector oven. When slightly brown put a thin slice of cheese between two crackers. Roast for a few minutes. The cheese will run over, under and around the crackers. Serve hot and boast, "It can't be beat!" Good for late afternoon with a cup of tea—or perhaps a bit "wild," but finally mild, hot buttered rum—but that's another story.

FIREPLACE CINNAMON TOAST

For a four o'clock tidbit, there is nothing equal to toasted white bread with cinnamon and sugar. First toast the bread, spread with butter, sprinkle with cinnamon and spread with sugar. Set back against the fire till the sugar gets hot and sizzles, the cinnamon spreads and your toast is ready. Add a cup of tea or coffee. It's a perfect four o'clock touch-off. Your guests will like it.

Rolled Roast of Beef
BEFORE THE FIREPLACE OR OPEN FIRE

Roast beef, either rib or rolled, needs constant turning before a reflector fire. Bind the roast with stovepipe wire, both ways, to hold it tightly together. Have one lead wire running up from the roast and fasten to a piece of twine or cord. This to provide for twisting. Fasten twine to top of fireplace shelf or on a pole in front of your open fire. On twine above wire place a cross-stick, ends of which run through the cord strand. These rest against the fire place wall. Turn this stick every five or ten minutes so the roast is exposed on all sides. With an outdoor fire a longer branch, say three feet long, can be applied to regulate the turning of the roast.

I forgot to mention the drip pan. Place a frying pan below the roast just in front of the reflector oven. (See sketch.) Place in this drip pan a bit of lemon, orange juice, cinnamon, cloves, butter, sugar and water enough to keep it watery. Soon the roast will begin to sizzle and drip into the drip pan below. With a long-handled spoon (fasten a three-foot wooden handle to a large tureen spoon) dip up the juice from the drip pan and baste the hot roast every

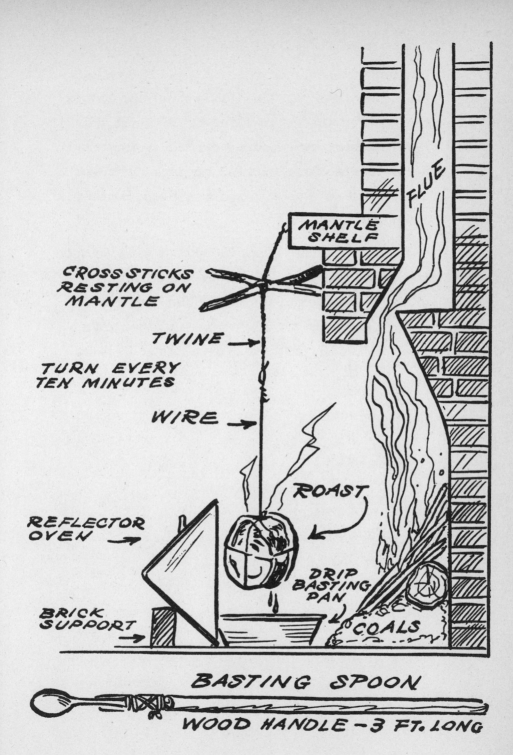

FLUE

MANTLE SHELF

CROSS STICKS RESTING ON MANTLE

TWINE →

TURN EVERY TEN MINUTES

WIRE →

ROAST

REFLECTOR OVEN →

DRIP BASTING PAN

BRICK SUPPORT →

COALS

BASTING SPOON

WOOD HANDLE — 3 FT. LONG

few minutes. Flames will flare up. Keep a hot fire. Don't worry. This is as it should be. Keep the fire very hot. An eight-pound roast will require about two hours. Gather around the fireplace—cushions, chairs, perhaps a bridge game—but watch the roast. Keep basting often.

When is it done? If you want a rare roast inside and burnt and crisp on the outside, the above will show you the way. The best way to really know is to try a few roasts of your own. You will finally find your own answer—rare, medium, well-done, burnt—or all at the same time.

THE SHORE DINNER

"A morsel for a Monarch"—Shakespeare

Do you really want a great meal full of anticipation—a meal that will keep you "drooling" for forty-five minutes as you watch its progress—a meal which in its stages of development will make you forget business, problems, worries, and when finished and eaten will leave you relaxed and in a happy daze of comfortable calm—a meal fit for kings, but which today may be enjoyed by vagabonds?

Are you really hungry and are you prepared to intrigue your palate with a real rare experience which after eating will leave your being satiated, contented, satisfied? Then try the "Lobster Pot"—lobsters, clams, clam broth, chicken, vegetables—all in one cooker the size of the family wash boiler. Indeed, the home wash boiler is just about right size to cook for a party up to ten people.

It is obvious being four to five hundred miles from the seashore (Buffalo, N. Y.) we must secure the best and freshest lobsters and clams possible. Through an arrangement that I have with a Boston shipper, we get lobsters delivered

CHICKEN
VEGETABLES
SEA WEED
LOBSTERS
TRAY
TRAY
TRAY
TRAY
CLAMS
SPIGOT
BROTH
FUEL →

BOTTOM
TRAY

90

here in Buffalo within fifteen hours after being caught.

The meal is a perfectly simple one; or it can be made elaborate. It is not an expensive meal. Most of all it needs a little dramatics—the out-of-door setting, the group near enough to the outdoor cooking to watch it casually as conversation leads to western civilization, war, peace and humdrum gossip—but observe all of the food items that are included—the stunning of the lobsters by a blow on the head and puncturing the brain with an ice pick—not pleasant but humane—green, fresh, live lobsters that come out of the pot a brilliant red.

The spigot on the lobster pot is not essential, but very convenient, for the first course is the serving of a cup of broth together with a big bowl of clams and drawn butter. Serve each person wherever they are sitting—on the grass, in garden chairs, etc. If the broth is really as it should be—that is, made up of all the drippings from the food within the cooker, your guests will want a second helping. So they go over to the cooker and draw from the spigot the steaming broth, without having to dip down deep into the cooker and risk the danger of burns from the steam.

Because I could not find the kind of equipment I wanted for my shore dinner, I had my own tank or lobster pot cooker made. It is nothing more than a tin tank, 16" x 16" x 16" with a somewhat snug fitting cover. Within are four wire basket trays that fit one on top of the other. They contain all the ingredients except bread, butter, salad, coffee and dessert.

Here is what to include—clams, lobsters, chicken (if you want to be lavish), celery, carrots, potatoes, sweet corn, green or wax beans, or any combination of fresh vegetables, and seaweed. The broth, clams and lobsters are the important part of the meal. You won't want to eat many vegetables—their importance is to flavor the broth.

But let's get on with the preparation—

(1) Pour a gallon and a half of water into the cooker. Bring to a wild boiling state—that is, there must be real steam generated in the cooker to the point where the cover will bob up and down and may need a small stone on top to keep it in place.

(2) Place the lobsters (preferably two-pound ones) in the second tray from the bottom; cover with seaweed.

(3) Place the cut-up chicken (broilers are preferable) in the next tray above. (Wrap each piece of chicken in cheese cloth. When the dinner is done the chicken should be white and mealy and will need to be pan-browned in butter. The cheese cloth will keep the meat from falling apart.) If there is any room in the tray add vegetables.

Note: The chicken is an extra and can be omitted.

(4) In the next tray above put all the rest of the vegetables. Sweet corn on the cob is most desirable and will do much to enrich the broth. (Note: Speaking of these trays, I have attached to the bottom tray a long wire handle running up on the inside of either side of the cooker so that all trays can be lifted out at one time. (A good pair of canvas gloves with cuffs is necessary to protect your hands and arms from the steam.)

(5) Put these four trays in the cooker and let steam for forty minutes. And, brother, I mean steam!

(6) At the end of the forty minutes lift out all trays and fill the bottom tray with clams. Put all trays back and steam for ten minutes longer. Your shore dinner will then be ready.

(7) Remove the cooker from the fire. Draw off the broth. Serve a bowl of clams to your guests with dishes of drawn butter. Eat the clam with your fingers and have plenty of towels or paper napkins on hand. Be prepared to decorate your face from ear to ear. One just may not be fastidious at this stage of the game.

(8) In the meantime place the trays on a table or bench and let your guests help themselves. It will be necessary, however, for some one to split the lobsters in halves after you have removed the seaweed. This is best done with a small hand-axe or cleaver, if you have one. One-half lobster to each person is ample.

(9) Now add a chef's salad, bread, butter, coffee and those other things you may want for your meal. For dessert there is nothing that I have found goes better than just half of a grapefruit. It cuts

through and brings one back to normal.

If you go to a cottage where you have tables, dishes and all of the other equipment, then, of course, it is nice to serve this shore dinner with a bit of more formality. As I said in the beginning, there is nothing unusual about this meal. Be sure to get seaweed when you buy your lobsters. Do not salt the chicken or you will spoil the tang of the seaweed. Seaweed will season it sufficiently. The chicken should be salted to taste when browned.

Another tip. Be sure to watch your broth that it does not boil away. You will have to determine the amount of water by the size of the cooker you have at your disposal. To me the best part of the meal is the clam broth. Save the left-over broth for lunch tomorrow.

FRONT

REFLECTOR OVEN BISCUITS

Do you know how to mix baking powder biscuits without using utensils and measuring tools No? Let me give you a man's outdoor 1-4-3-2-1 method.

Take a hand full of flour (as much as your cupped hand will hold). Put in a dish or small pail, if you do this at home. If on the hike, put it in a washed five-pound salt bag. Now dip your fingers and thumb drawn to a point, into the baking powder can and draw out as much baking powder as your fingers and thumb will hold. It won't be much, but it will be enough. Next pick up as much salt as you can pick up with three fingers and your thumb and throw into the "kitty" (bag). Your next move is to pick up all the sugar you can with two fingers and the thumb. Add this to the bag. Finally stick your index finger into a jar of shortening and withdraw as much as you can up to the first knuckle. You now have the ingredients for one big biscuit. If you want two or more, increase the process to the size and number of biscuits you want. Add milk, or if milk is not available, water and mix to a stiff paste. Sprinkle a bit of flour on a piece of paper, flatten your biscuit and cut into inch and a half squares. Place in reflector oven pan and place reflector oven close to hot fire. After a few minutes turn biscuits around so as to bake on both sides. Now get a real taste of the sunny south. Serve with butter and jam.

YOUR COMPLETE DINNER ON TWO STICKS OF WOOD

A delicious meal can be cooked on two sticks of wood. Beef, mutton or lamb—onion, bacon, biscuits, plus potatoes baked in the coals, a cup of cocoa and an apple—a real meal, without any cooking utensils—just a cup for the cocoa. Do you want to try it in your garden? Well, I have explained the importance of a good bed of coals which is vital in any outdoor pioneer cooking venture.

This meal is simple. Cut a straight branch of dry wood the thickness of your thumb, and about two-feet long, preferably white pine. Some wood is bitter (like oak), some sweet. The way to find out is to taste it. If it tastes bitter, then certainly it isn't sweet—so avoid it. With your jackknife whittle your stick smooth and cut a sharp point at one end.

Now cut your meat into one and one-half inch squares. Cut bacon slices to same size. Cut onions cross-wise so you will have many rings. Next push the pointed end of stick through a piece of meat, then a piece of bacon, then a ring of onion. Do this again and again

98

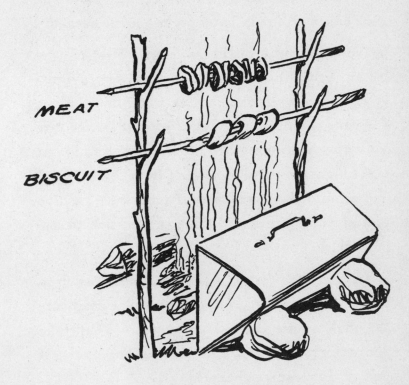

MEAT

BISCUIT

99

until you have at least a quarter-pound of meat or more, according to your appetite—first meat, then bacon, then onion until the stick is filled. Leave an eighth-inch o f space between each piece. Salt and pepper. (If you really want a pioneer salt and pepper shaker, take a piece of your old bamboo fishing pole. Cut off two inches on either side of the joint. Fill one end with salt, the other with pepper. Put a cork in each end and put in your pocket until needed.)

Now we come to the real fun. Prepare the biscuit using the 1-4-3-2-1 method as previously explained. Secure another stick like the one for your meat. Flatten your biscuit batter into a long ribbon about two inches wide and about eight inches long and one-half inch thick. Wind this around the second stick barber-pole fashion and pinch at either end tight to the stick to seal it in place.

(Be sure to start to bake your potatoes first, because they take longer. Put them deep into the coals or use the reflector oven. They take about forty minutes and time is important if you want to serve everything hot.)

Cut two branches about two feet long with small branches sticking out at side and tip to hold your two sticks. (See illustration.) Force these into the ground on either side of hot coals. Place the meat stick on top crotch. Give it a quarter turn every five minutes. Soon it will begin to sizzle. The fat from the bacon will run into the beef and the onion will curl up and brown and flavor your meat. Now place your biscuit stick on the crotch below and likewise give it a quarter-turn every few minutes. Soon it will begin to swell and then brown. (Stop "drooling!" Wait a bit longer.) Next the juice from the meat and bacon above will drip down on your biscuit and you will have buttered hot biscuit.

Set your cup of cocoa near the fire, unwrap the celery, radishes—shine up the apple for your dessert—and presto, you have prepared a royal meal.

Throw all the waste into the fire,
Take home the cup and now aspire
To simpler life and greater giving.
You, too, will grow by simple living.

Lamps, Lighting and Illumination

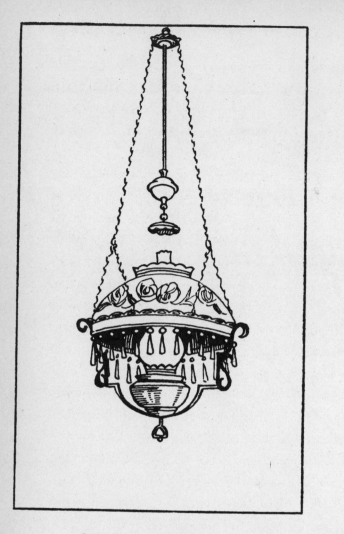

104

Lamps, Lighting and Illumination

KEROSENE lamps are almost a luxury in this day of electricity. They throw long flickering shadows—so do candles. Log cabins are intimately associated with candles and kerosene lamps.

Chain-pull kerosene lamps can still be bought from second-hand stores or antique shops. I wish I could find again the beautiful hanging lamp of my boyhood days. Way back in the nineties, as I remember, it seemed there were a "thousand" crystals hanging around the globe dome. We pulled it down over the living room table, back on the farm when the family gathered after supper and the day's work was done. A dish of apples supplied from our cellar, also a dish of hickory nuts. One of the older members of the family would crack the nuts on the bottom of the old-fashioned flatiron— the kind that mother used to heat by placing it on the top of the kitchen stove on ironing day. The real family life was around the living room table, under the dome of our chain-pull crystal-decorated lamp. Here was security—the peace and quiet companionship of the family.

The wagon wheel "chandelier" suspended from the roof-ridge with logging chains is a modern interpretation; yet it conforms with the spirit of the Cabin-in-the-Woods. Place either lamps or candles on the rim. Here is room to follow your own fancy.

LANTERN MAGIC

What an important part the lantern has played in American pioneer life. Within the squared-oak log cabin back on the farm in Wisconsin, winter nights closed in at four or five o'clock in the afternoon. As we approached the barn to do the chores, our lantern cast great shadows of the person ahead of us on the barn wall—shadows which grew larger and larger with each approaching step, until they became giant-sized. Inside the barn the lantern was hung on a wooden peg. Each person sat on a milking stool, head pressed against the belly of a cow, pail gripped between the knees. As each pail became full we would carry the warm milk near to the lantern, pour its contents through a clean-washed cloth strainer into the milk can and return to the next cow for the second ten quarts. One cow I milked had the habit of switching her tail in my direction so I remember I would place her tail between my head and the side of her belly and press hard. The smell of cow dung, animal odor, the warm moisture of the barn, the smell of sweet hay and the pungent odor of silo feed were a part of pioneer American life.

The lantern, as it cast its feeble flickering rays, was an important part of the milking ceremony. It was the only light we had.

Lanterns cast soft lights. Their "feeble" shadows teach you patience and calm. You find in them a slowing-down process. They help to take you from high tension back to a wholesome normal. Try it. You, too, will discover magic in the old-fashioned lantern.

106

"THE CELLAR MYSTERY"

Taking the lantern into the cellar was the prize experience of my day on the farm. After the day's work was done and the family gathered in the living room for an hour's companionship and the sharing of the day's experiences and gossip, it was my job to light the lantern and go to the cellar for apples, nuts, a piece of homemade cheese.

Lanterns as well as lamps in those days were kept in shining condition. Each morning all lamps and lanterns were refilled with kerosene out in the woodshed. They were then placed on the shelf or in their hangers only after wicks had been trimmed, chimneys washed in soapy water and polished to a shining brightness.

And so I would pull down the lever of the lantern, strike a sulphur match, let it burn for a minute until its pungent fumes were spent, then light the lantern, raise the lever and adjust the wick so it would not smoke. Then I would proceed to the cellar.

There is a smell about the farm cellar that always gave me a feeling of contentment and security. Down—down—down—step by step into the black void—my feeble light pushing back the darkness, but also revealing queer forms and shapes waiting silently. Their swaying shadows cast on the white-washed stone walls would move in the rhythm of the lantern motion. To stand in the middle of this almost magic storehouse, while my eyes accustomed themselves to the lantern light as I hung it on its wooden peg, gave me both shivers and delight. No modern furnace in this cellar. The heating stoves were upstairs. It was always a bit chilly—a damp, earthy smell mingled with the sweet smell of apples—Duchess, Red Astrachans, Russets, Snow apples. How I loved them! Each shiny apple reflected a pearly spot from the light of the lantern.

Next were two fifty-gallon cider vinegar barrels—one with a "mother" that was in the making; the other with ripened cider vinegar There were two barrels of real cider which was brought up in big pitcherfuls on Sundays or special occasions.

Shall I ever forget mother's ten-gallon pickle jar? The big bin of potatoes—forty bushels or more; the salt pork barrel; pickled pigs feet; the shelf of homemade hand cheese and cottage cheese. Then the shelf of big stone bowls of milk from which each morning the cream was skimmed. Cabbages, beets, carrots, rutabaga, kohlrabi—all packed in sand bins. In the corner stood the ice cream freezer—idle, until brought out for those summer picnics and Sundays. Overhead hung huge slabs of bacon and smoked hams. Also there was the cupboard of two hundred or more jars of preserves, vegetables and jams.

Those were hard-working days, but happy ones. And when the winter came and the storms blew, the lantern would light the way to that cellar of security. Here fruits of our labors were reflected in the lantern light which dispelled darkness and the thought of insecurity.

Tricks
of the
Trade

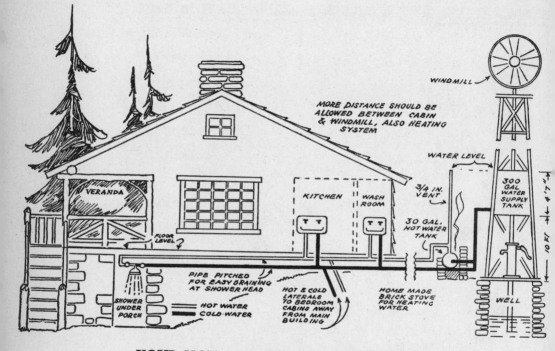

Labels within the illustration:

WINDMILL

MORE DISTANCE SHOULD BE
ALLOWED BETWEEN CABIN
& WINDMILL, ALSO HEATING
SYSTEM

WATER LEVEL

3/4 IN.
VENT

30 GAL.
HOT WATER
TANK

300
GAL.
WATER
SUPPLY
TANK

10 FT.   4 FT.

VERANDA

KITCHEN

WASH
ROOM

FLOOR
LEVEL

PIPE PITCHED
FOR EASY DRAINING
AT SHOWER HEAD

SHOWER
UNDER
PORCH

HOT WATER
COLD WATER

HOT & COLD
LATERALS
TO BEDROOM
CABINS AWAY
FROM MAIN
BUILDING

HOME MADE
BRICK STOVE
FOR HEATING
WATER

WELL

YOUR HOT AND COLD WATER SYSTEM
AND SUPPLY

Tricks of the Trade

RUNNING HOT AND COLD WATER

A summer camp is incomplete without a shower bath. One does not need to think in terms of tile floors or granite bath tubs. A hot and cold water system can be installed for very little cost. In fact we built one which supplied hot and cold water to not only the shower, but also for the kitchen and washroom. Except for the pump and windmill we built it for less than ten dollars. It was fun to work with stilson wrenches, valves, fittings, water pressure, air vents, et cetera.

A housewrecking company supplied sinks, pipes, valves at very reasonable cost. A thirty-gallon hot water tank laid flat with a fire hole under it resulted in our hot water heating system. A wood fire built in it in the morning would smolder all day and keep water hot. On sunny days we had a solar heating system with no effort or expense. Three oak barrels connected by pipe will store one hundred and fifty gallons of water.

Careful study of "Your Hot and Cold Water System and Supply" tells its own story.

Waste

"JOHNNIES" AND INCINERATORS

Toilets at their best are none too good. Most toilets in the woods smell; are a disturbance. If you insist on having a toilet inside your cabin, then you must follow certain precautions.

There are, generally speaking, three kinds of toilets—flush, septic, old-fashioned privies.

FLUSH TOILETS

If in your Cabin-in-the-Woods you can have running water and proper drainage, and if you can keep running water from freezing, then install flush toilet inside your cabin; also shower bath, as well as kitchen running water. In the far south this may be in keeping and successful. To go to your cabin on week-ends in the winter where temperature gets below freezing, you have at once a different problem. Unless you can properly shut off all water below frost line and also drain all receptacles, you will have no end of trouble and inconvenience. This, then is a problem for your plumber.

SEPTIC

Septic systems (bacteria action) can be installed inside your cabin, but you will not be pleased with the results. They give off an odor of some kind or another. On a warm still night they exude fumes (sweet sickly smell) that remind you constantly of the presence of a toilet within your cabin. This kind of toilet is most successful fifty or one hundred feet or more away from your cabin. Observe local state health laws. (You will, however, find them efficient, economical.)

PRIVIES

The old-fashioned privy or "backhouse" is still a good type of outdoor toilet if properly built. First the pit must be deep (five or six feet at least). Secondly, properly boxed—a fly-proof seat and cover. The seat-cover should be so constructed that it drops in place automatically. The building should be fly-proof and screened. This toilet should be at least fifty feet from the cabin; better one hundred or one hundred and fifty feet away, and by all means away from any possible drainage towards your spring or well. Consult your local health authorities.

YOU DECIDE

It is now for you to decide where you want your toilet; according to your desires and within your means and health regulations. A "one hole" backyard privy can be built for as low as ten dollars for material if you do the work.

Even an outdoor toilet can be built along good lines. Paint or stain it to fit into the surrounding color scheme. Plant young trees or vines to enclose it.

INCINERATORS

This subject may seem unimportant, except for the necessity of a simple daily disposal and avoidance of odors about your cabin. I have tried several kinds—wire frames, stone incinerators, et cetera. What is most needed is an efficient method of getting rid of daily waste that naturally accumulates in a cabin—waste paper, tin cans, garbage.

I have found a plain open pit the simplest of all—a pit three feet deep by five feet in diameter. As you dig the pit throw up a bank of dirt three feet wide all around the pit. This will raise a wall all around and will protect you against grass fires when you burn the refuse. Wrap garbage in paper; helps in the combustion. Throw in small branches of waste wood. Build a fire in the pit and burn the refuse. If damp, spray with creosote solution which will keep the flies away. A pit used this way will serve a year for six people. It then needs cleaning out; or dig a new pit and cover the old one.

One word of caution—be sure to so place the pit that the prevailing winds will carry odors and smoke away from your cabin.

THE OIL DRUM INCINERATOR

Dig a trench eight inches deep by ten inches wide and ten feet long. Now dig another at right angles to cross the center—same length. Place an oil drum in the center, open top and with large two-inch holes punched in the bottom. You can do this with an old axe. The four trenches will carry the prevailing wind from any of four directions and travel up the oil drum. Throw waste paper and garbage in the drum and let it burn. If garbage is balanced with paper and other inflammable material, your incinertor will smolder all day and gradually burn out. Occasionally dump the ashes, bottles, glass and other solid material.

OTHER WASTE

Much that we throw away in the city is well worth saving in the woods—string, twine, paper from wrappings, small boxes and cartons. You may find it more difficult to run to the store to replenish your needs. You will fully realize this, once you are "caught short."

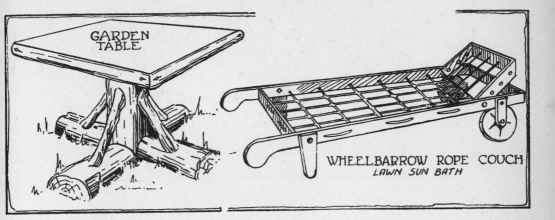

GARDEN TABLE

WHEELBARROW ROPE COUCH
LAWN SUN BATH

RUSTIC FURNITURE

Rustic furniture inside or out will add more than anything to the artistry and homelikeness of your camp. It is by no means difficult if built of natural rustic material because every piece of natural wood has graceful lines. However roughly fashioned, your articles will be good looking. Rope, some bolts, a few nails, a good sharp axe, an expansion bit for boring one-inch to one and one-half inch holes, a draw shave, small timber from the woods, two to four inches in diameter, and a little ingenuity are all that are needed. The illustrations may be followed exactly or make your own adaptation to suit your fancy.

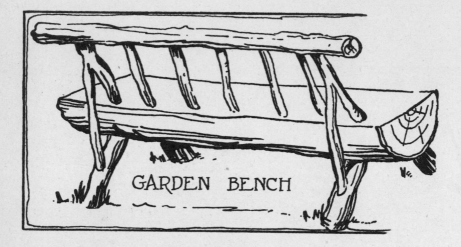

GARDEN BENCH

THE HALF-LOG BENCH

Cut six-foot logs from a fourteen to eighteen-inch tree. Split through the middle. Bore four holes one and one-half inch at angle in the bottom or round-part of log so that peglegs will protrude from seat "fore and aft" about four inches. Back-rest needs one and one-half inch holes with support running to back legs. The seat part should be dressed, planed and sandpapered.

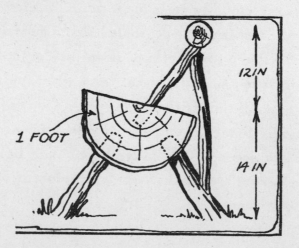

1 FOOT

12 IN

14 IN

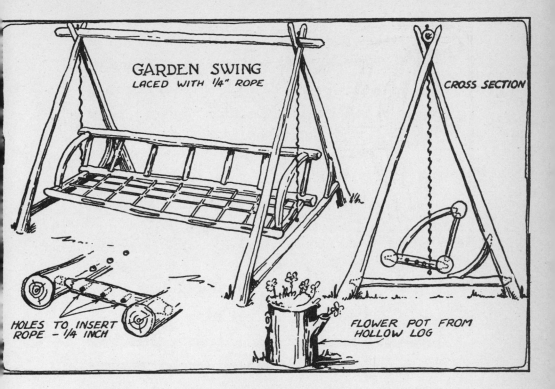

GARDEN SWING
LACED WITH 1/4" ROPE

CROSS SECTION

HOLES TO INSERT
ROPE - 1/4 INCH

FLOWER POT FROM
HOLLOW LOG

THE RUSTIC HAMMOCK
OR GARDEN SWING

Six feet six inches long, it will serve as a bed. Canvas over frame will serve as tent and makes good extra bed when the unexpected visitor arrives. Start with seat frame. The two end pins doweled into long ends. Then bore holes every four inches all around and lace with one-quarter inch rope. Homemade cushions will serve as mattress and seat. Try corn-shucks for mattress. Just fill a straw tick with hand-picked corn shucks. They make a very comfortable bed. Use the soft springy inner part of corn husk. Outer leaves are harsh.

ROPE BUNKS

Make good cabin beds. Bore three-eighth inch holes every four inches around frame of four-inch saplings. Lace with one-quarter inch rope. Bunks with slats on which to place springs and mattresses make good beds.

CHEST UNDER BUNKS

Serves well for storage and utility space. Casters under chest make easy handling.

STORM DOORS

It will help your heating problem in winter, if you add storm doors to your cabin. I have seen a cabin with picnic table with folding legs fitted as storm door in winter, but in summer unhinged and again used as picnic table.

TRICK DOOR WITH SECRET LOCK

What could be more discouraging than to arrive at your winter cabin after a long hike, cold and a bit wet, to find you have forgotten the key to your cabin. Here is a cure for that human weakness, at least protection against it. A trick door lock. Pull a leather thong, push a slide, lift a latch, and presto, the door opens! Work out your own combination. Make it as complicated as your imagination suggests, but don't forget the combination.

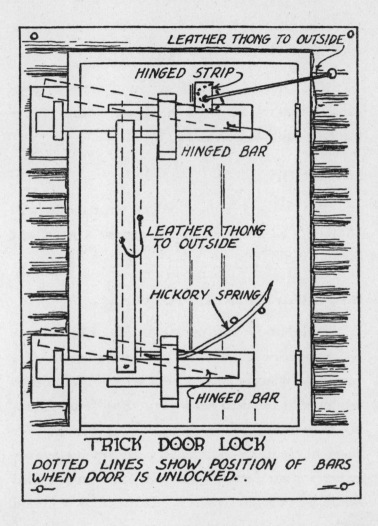

LEATHER THONG TO OUTSIDE

HINGED STRIP

HINGED BAR

LEATHER THONG TO OUTSIDE

HICKORY SPRING

HINGED BAR

TRICK DOOR LOCK

DOTTED LINES SHOW POSITION OF BARS WHEN DOOR IS UNLOCKED.

TRIM PLATE DECORATION

A decorative effect can be given by dressing plates with half-round four-inch or split logs.

WOODEN PEG COAT HANGERS

Coat hangers can be made of wooden pegs three-quarters of an inch thick. Bore three-quarter inch holes in log.

SKY LIGHT

A sky light in the roof of your cabin will add light on dark days. It is also a good out for hot air.

NATURAL ICE BOX COOLER

Build an ice box cooler in side of hill. Stone walls on sides and back. Top dome-shaped. Use two inch by eight inch frame with double doors inside and out. Will keep vegetables from freezing in winter; cellar coolness in summer. Or build an eighteen-inch by eighteen-inch elevator cellar within your cabin, five feet deep. This raised by rope and pulley. It must be supplied with outside drainage on down side of hill.

THE FRAME HOUSE –

Thus far we have discussed log cabins along very simple lines. Something now should be said for frame buildings for the person who loves the out-of-doors, but who prefers to erect a bit more modern building. Modern in the sense that he prefers plastered walls inside and painted walls without. A white cottage with green blinds. Why not? I must admit I could not treat this subject with any such warmth and length as I would the lore that surrounds log cabins. Nor is it necessary. There is unlimited source material on the subject of frame buildings.

These drawings may help you. A local carpenter can be of real help. He will help you to figure the amount of lumber with accuracy and without waste; also length of plates, rafters, joists—windows and board feet of lumber to complete the job. More than this he can help you build it and with speed.

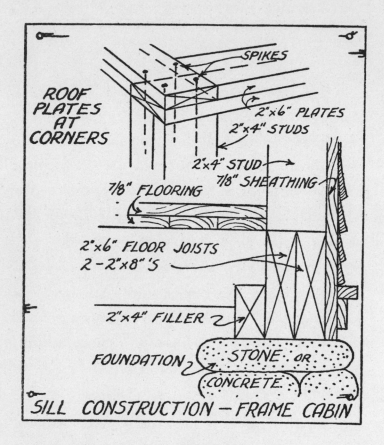

Diagram labels: SPIKES; ROOF PLATES AT CORNERS; 2"x6" PLATES; 2"x4" STUDS; 2"x4" STUD; 7/8" SHEATHING; 7/8" FLOORING; 2"x6" FLOOR JOISTS 2 - 2"x8" 'S; 2"x4" FILLER; FOUNDATION; STONE OR CONCRETE; SILL CONSTRUCTION — FRAME CABIN

ROOF PLATES AT CORNERS

Here we have plates at top of studding fastened at corners, also sill construction on foundation. To keep your cabin warm underfoot it is well to build a double floor filled in between with tar paper.

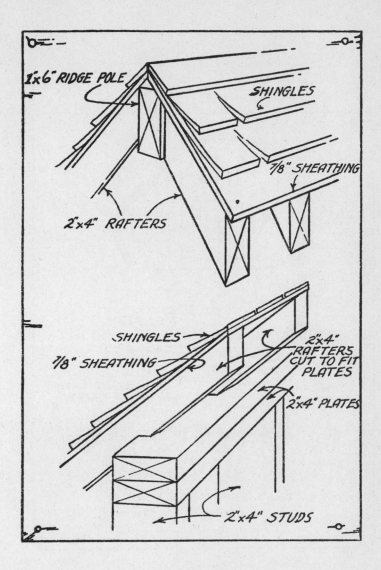

Above gives construction of roof rafters and method of fastening.

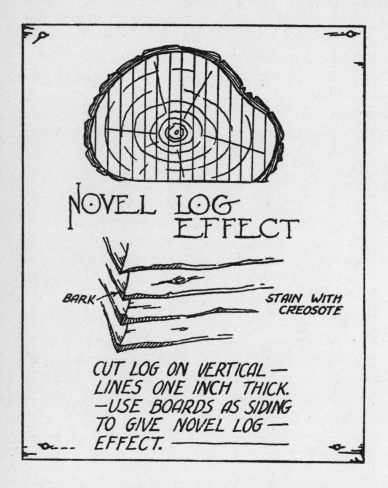

NOVEL LOG EFFECT

BARK

STAIN WITH CREOSOTE

CUT LOG ON VERTICAL —
LINES ONE INCH THICK.
—USE BOARDS AS SIDING
TO GIVE NOVEL LOG —
EFFECT. ———

NOVEL LOG EFFECTS

If you want your house to look rustic you can get a clever log effect on your frame building by ripping one-inch boards off logs, going straight through the bark. After one slab is removed from the log, turn log over to rest flat on the table of the saw. Then one after the other, boards are ripped off. This gives you a rough edge with a strip of bark and gives you somewhat the outline of a log. Use these as clapboards with the bark end to the bottom. Cut these logs in summer or fall when there is no sap in the trees.

FLAG STONE FLOORS

If you really want a warm snug cabin, free from floor drafts, free from sweat, rich in design and colorful beyond what even an inlaid floor would give, then build a flagstone floor for your cabin. Surprisingly, too, you will find the stone warmer than a wood floor.

Did you ever warm up a cabin in severe winter weather and notice the painted floor sweat great beads of moisture as the fires got under way? A flagstone floor properly laid will not do this. In fact it will start getting warm as soon as you build a fire and will stay warm. This because the floor is dry and does not absorb moisture.

A flagstone floor needs first a foundation built all around the cabin and below frost line —four feet or better in New York State, less as you go farther south. Anchor the first log or plate to the foundation with bolts buried in the cement at least eight inches. Drainage on the outside of the cabin—that is, the ground pitches down and away from the building at least eighteen inches. Lay four to six inches of gravel within your cabin and four inches below top of concrete foundation. Upon this lay your flagstone floor. After it is laid and leveled, pour a soupy, strong mixture of cement in between the flagstones. This is commonly called "grouting."

If you do not have flat stones on your property, you can get pieces of marble, slate, et cetera, from your housewrecking or construction company. Since the first log is anchored to the foundation, there is no need of binding with floor joists as in the case of a wooden floor.

Manufactured stepping stones may seem a bit incongruous and artificial; yet I know of places where there are no flat stones for building paths, trails or stepping stones. I had a lot of fun once when building a cabin site in wild country where rocks were of the molten kind and I just could not get a flat surface. Then why have flat stones? Now I determined to have them; so having enough sand and cement we made them. We learned some interesting things in this experiment.

First we built pans two inches deep out of scrap sheet iron. We finally agreed on five patterns, each different so that they could be fitted together in several ways. We had some red sandstone chips from our fireplace, also pieces of blue and red marble. We broke these in pieces the size of hickory nuts and mixed them in the cement, and then poured the mixture into the forms. After the cement mixture "set" we

126

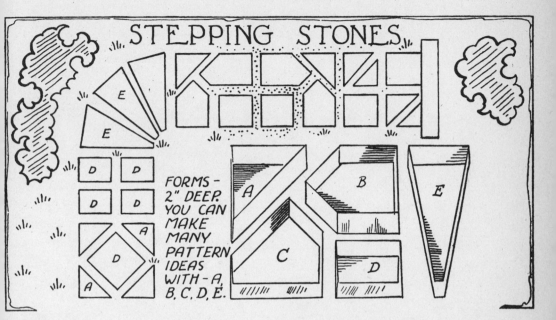

STEPPING STONES

FORMS – 2" DEEP. YOU CAN MAKE MANY PATTERN IDEAS WITH – A, B, C, D, E.

smoothed the top surface with a trowel. After two days we removed the cement blocks and rubbed them down with a common brick. To our amazement the chips of sandstone and marble gave the cement block a really natural appearance. Still more interesting, after a month or two they weathered into soft colors that fitted quite naturally into the setting.

Be sure to rub oil on the inside of your pans before pouring in the cement or you may have difficulty in removing the blocks.

Personality
Plus

Put

Personality

Plus

INTO ALL YOU CREATE

THE story is told of three masons who were doing the same kind of work. A passerby inquired of each mason, "What are you doing?" "I'm laying brick," said the first mason. "I'm building a wall," the second man answered. The third mason in answer to the same question replied, "I'm building a great cathedral." Certainly no one will question which of the three masons lived the fuller life.

And so, Mr. Cabin-Builder, I challenge you to build a "cathedral"—your greatest dream, when you create your Cabin-in-the-Woods. Be there woods or no; be it treeless as the Kansas prairies or the highest peaks of the Rockies— build into your cabin spot your loftiest thinking. You've got it. Think it through. It will bless you and yours if you resort not to just "laying brick or building a wall."

Put personality-plus into all you create.

What Shall I Wear?

SUMMER TOGS

Summer in northern zones comes and goes all too quickly. The lover of the outdoors will naturally take advantage of the daily sun bath. I've heard it called "Vitamin D." The youngsters as well as grown-ups grow rugged and take on that dark brown color that fits into the outdoors. Here is the time and place to dress, or shall I say undress, down to bare necessities. The best looking summer suit is the sun tan with just enough dress so as not to shock Aunt Maria.

WINTER TOGS

A plaid wool shirt, a bit gaudy in color; lots of red, expressing warmth. Necktie to reflect one's personality, whim or mood. Corduroy trousers—green, purple or brown—to make a bold contrast. A belt of one's own handicraft—heavy shoes or laced boots. A lumberjack coat of many colors—warm, snug at the neck. Let the winds blow! A bit of rain in the face and like it. A cap with visor and earlaps. Hail the modern pioneer! Who wants to stay inside and warm his shins?

There is work to do. Wood to haul. Water to carry. The garden wall to be built. It will harden your hands, toughen your muscles—a bit of natural sweat. So open your coat, breathe deeply. It's got it all over a steam bath. A town steam bath and rub-down as a regular diet is plain organized idleness with a thrill, which develops the attendant's muscles, but leaves you soft, flabby — a perfect parlor camper.

This is the great outdoors, elemental life —shadows lengthen—day is done—wholesome fatigue—and now a bit of rest and the fireplace —reflection, supper — contentment. Outside the wind is whining. The nights grow cold— the cabin is warm—flickering shadows from the cheery fireplace—stillness—quiet.

A wool shirt, no longer gaudy in color, fits into the setting. Woolly slippers. A Cabin-in-the-Woods—the elements—a companion who understands. We light our pipes—fragrant tobacco—the world goes by—somehow cabin togs are appropriate.

SKILL TO DO IT ONESELF

After your cabin plans are completed, build a miniature cabin. If you are unfamiliar with reading blue prints, the miniature cabin will prove most helpful. More than this, it will serve as a perfect guide, save errors and also expense.

Every person who has ever built a house of any kind says without fail, "If I were to build again . . . " No great project was ever built before a model was built, in order to visualize to the unskilled mind just what it would look like. So with us the building field is new and we need to proceed carefully. More than this, with a model we can get a better perspective by a little adjustment here, raising or lowering the roof, by extending the eaves—to give it graceful lines. You don't want your cabin to look like a garage when it is finished.

You will become so thoroughly familiar with every piece of log or lumber—its dimension and fitting—used in your cabin that you will approach the real building with confidence and sound enjoyment.

Build your miniature cabin one inch to the foot. In the winter in your workshop you will find this an ideal hobby. Whittle the logs of soft white pine about three-quarters of an inch in diameter. Use thin packing boxes for lumber and cut to size. Your hardware store will supply you with one-quarter inch and one-half inch brads for nails. Leave the roof removable, so you can look inside and plan for the rooms. Build tiny bookracks, lockers, beds, et cetera, your table and rustic chairs and build them to scale. Have the family or members interested check each item with you. Re-arrange doors and windows to your liking. Check space and if unsatisfactory, make changes. Then you won't be disappointed or wish you had done it differently. When erecting your cabin, take the miniature along. It will serve as a blue print or better.

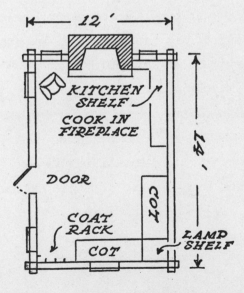

SIGN POSTS AND TRAIL MARKERS

In the early days of our country, when our forefathers were struggling with the building of a great democracy, among other things a certain culture and refinement were finding their place in American life. Virginia planters gave evidence of this new budding culture. A colored boy was stationed at the gateway to bid the wayfarer welcome. Many a weary guest looked with favor upon this welcome and entered the portals of kindliness to be received by gracious hosts, to spend the night, to exchange the latest news—to be on his way early on the morrow.

The colored boy at the gate was a sign or symbol of the friendliness and courtesy of his master's household. You can carry this friendly spirit of pioneer America into your cabin building.

Does the name you have chosen for your camp site — "Camp Elizabeth," or "Shady Pines," or a bit flippantly, "Dew Drop Inn," express your welcome to your friends and neighbors? Does it say, "We want you to come and share with us what we have? We delight in your coming."?

Express your personality in some sign or symbol—perhaps a pine tree cut out of metal, your name fashioned in rustic wood, a novel wrought-iron lantern. Your sign or symbol will not only represent the name of your place, but the character of the people within.

My daughter Betty Ellen adds

Let "Mother Nature"

BE YOUR GARDENER

One of the luxuries of a Cabin-in-the-Woods is the abundance of nearby wild flowers. Wild flowers complete the personality of gentle slopes, rugged steeps and lush flatlands. No need of "green fingers" or a knowledge of gardening processes to have a wild garden in the country. You have the soil, sun and moisture necessary to the flowers in your neighborhood.

If you want a more formal garden than the changing patchwork of fields beyond the windows, start with a scrap of lawn, a field stone terrace, or a rough fence.

To form a backdrop in our garden we have transplanted clumps of goldenrod, pepper plant from the fields and built a loose framework of branches upon which woodbine climbs thick and green. Before it, daisies, purple-bell flowers and brown-eyed susans are happily grouped. Down the slope in a swampy hollow are wild iris, butter-yellow cowslips, forget-me-nots, tall day lilies and woods fern. A trickle from a spring furnishes a pool to mirror water lilies.

Let your garden infringe upon the lawn without corners or edges or too careful trimming. Tuck tiny plants between the stones of your walk or terrace. Leave the hillocks and hollows. Accentuate them with your planting. It should look as though it had just happened.

When you are strolling watch for an unusual plant. Dig it up with care. Tie it in your kerchief to plant on your return. Try to recreate the mood of its natural setting. Space these treasure-hunts throughout the summer and your garden will follow a natural sequence of bloom, for wild flowers are the hardiest of perennials.

You can let your garden grow lazily or you can become a connoisseur—searching out rare specimens. Our "show pieces" are cardinal flowers, showy lady-slippers and a flowering dogwood. Many cultivated plants slip in among the wild ones with ease, for they are merely wild flowers with a bit of education. Hollyhocks will spread in a few years to make charming splashes of color about the garden. Goldenglow, delphinium and phlox make friends with wild flowers in bouquets, for, of course, most gardens pre-suppose flowers within the house.

Flower arranging may be a simple part of the morning routine. Water lilies and their pads in a shallow pottery dish make a lovely centerpiece. Try a spray of goldenrod and a curve of half-ripe choke cherries over the fireplace. Pack daisies tightly in a small round bowl like an old-fashioned nosegay. Tall orange day-lilies will pay a compliment to an old bean jug.

The variety of wild flowers and their abundance are a daily challenge to expressing one's personality and mood. Even on rainy mornings some member of the family will always enjoy bundling into a slicker and rain-hat, to tramp through the tall grass and gather dripping color to make dark gray days friendly within and fresh with the woods' smell.

You may add all this variety of color to your cabin site without having to be a student of flowers. Flowers add richness and joy and interest in living. Try a wild flower garden and let Mother Nature be your gardener.

SHRUBS, TREES AND REFORESTATION

Raise your own forest. Plant tree seedlings and God will raise them. Plant them now. Trees are comparatively cheap as one or two-year-old seedlings. Plant five hundred each year for ten years. You can plant five hundred seedlings with the help of a man in less than a day. Carolina poplars grow fast. They will be thirty feet high in ten years' time and give generous shade. You will revel each year in their added growth.

Plant trees native to your territory—soft wood for fast growth. You can dig up quaking or saw-tooth aspens most anywhere. They will grow on the poorest kind of land. Conifers can be secured from your state forestry schools —white, red and jack pines, spruce. Would you like a ski course on your ranch? If so, plant red pines to arrest the snow on the windward side and add to your skiing and tobogganing.

Visualize the shade you will enjoy at the spot where you will have a perfect vista. Why not set out an orchard? Buy ten varieties of apple trees (fifty cents each); include a cherry tree, crabapple and one or two plum trees. You won't have to wait ten years for these to bear fruit. Add several nut trees, hickory, walnut or any trees suitable to the climate you live in.

Perhaps you want a winding road to your cabin spot. Here again you may need trees so that at each turn there may be added charm: first pines, then hemlocks, birch. Don't fail to plant some oaks—pin oaks, red oaks, sturdy oaks. Plant them from acorns. No cost except a little effort. I planted an acorn twenty years ago just for fun. Today it is the pride of all my planting. It is now twenty-five feet high. Who knows, you may live to enjoy those plantings of your earlier days and derive peace and joy each year you live to greet them. Please, please, do not make the usual mistake of saying, "I won't live long enough to enjoy the fruits of my labors." Plant those trees this year—today— whether you are thirty, fifty or seventy years old. They will bring you the richest returns.

Your Cabin-in-the-Woods, if you plan with vision, will become a cabin in the woods, even though you have started on a bare hillside. Plant trees. God will do most of the work. But plant them now!

Tune in on the Birds

BIRDS will come to your cabin and sing for you, if you encourage them. Feed and house them and their songs will gladden your heart. If you are unfamiliar with bird life you will soon discover a new interest and hobby. But more than this, your Cabin-in-the-Woods will become enchanted—a rendezvous for birds.

Build a rustic, simple feeding station. Build a box of half-inch wire mesh, fill it with suet occasionally and then watch the fun.

Besides giving us abounding pleasure in song and color, birds have a real economic value and your interest in and conservation of bird life is important. Birds protect vegetation which is so necessary for man's very existence. Some birds "police" the grounds, some the tree trunks, others the branches and leaves and still others the air—all devouring the destructive grubs and insects that would despoil our vegetation. Without vegetation our streams would dry up; without our water supply the human race would not exist. A small effort on your part to attract the birds will be a contribution toward all mankind.

Before winter is over, try to erect bird-houses for bluebirds, wrens and martins. Plant, if you can, thick clumps of bushes for catbirds and chirping sparrows, a trumpet vine for the humming bird and a mulberry tree for later joy of midsummer birds.

The spring migration starts in late February and lasts until June. It is a thrilling experience to keep count of the different kinds of birds that visit you. A good bird reference book and a pair of field glasses will help you identify your visitors from other climates and other lands.

In the fall put out feeding stations. While our wintering birds are relatively few, the chickadee and the downey and hairy wood-peckers and the nuthatches will come to feast near your windows throughout the winter months. For the effort made to attract and be-friend the birds that come to your locality, I know of no other reward so gratifying. If you must have a pet house-cat, provide her with a collar and small bell, so that the birds will have a fair chance to save themselves when the cat is abroad. This simple remedy to bird destruction is one big step toward success in being the "good neighbor" to your birds. The soft tinkle of the bell will alarm the birds no matter how carefully puss creeps up on them.

Birds will bring music to your cabin.

· TOLL · GATE ·

GATEWAYS, GUARD RAILS
FENCES AND FRIENDLINESS

As we pass through the gateway of our camp once the gate is closed, we are alone within. A closed gate implies privacy and the stranger will not intrude incautiously. However, too many people look upon a gate as a means of shutting out. Let us remember that the old gate swings in as well as out, bidding you welcome and inviting you to come again.

As far as history records, gateways depicted the personality of peoples and much of the art of the age. In the Roman days when warriors returned from triumphant battles, they

PIONEER

GARRISON

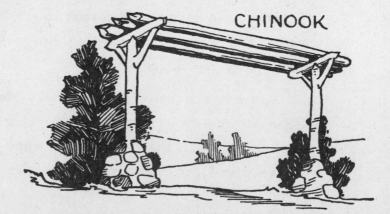

CHINOOK

146

were formally met by the governor or high priest at the gateway of the city and here welcomed and honored. In ancient times great cities were enclosed with high stone walls. Pretentious gateways were provided for the inhabitants to come and go on their peaceful pursuits. On state occasions the gateway to a city was the formal meeting place; the place for salutations; the crossing of swords. Lords and ladies were dressed in their finest—deep curtsies—sly flirtations—clicking of heels—salutes. In a word, the town was celebrating and came to its gateway to welcome honored guests and heroes.

ALAMO

WESTERN

In more modern days gateways still hold an important part in our communal life. What a thrill on arriving in one of our great cities to step off a train and into a beautiful, yes, by its very bigness, inspiring railway station. This is a modern city's gateway for its friends and inhabitants.

Now we are inside your gateway and following a winding road with changing vistas at each turn. The bank is steep on one side so a guard rail is on the curve to guide our guests who may walk or drive in the night—whitewashed boulders or perhaps a sign or symbol to give them direction.

As you enter the cabin door the mat may have the word "Welcome" woven into it. Often wrought-iron lamps on either side of the door light your way and add welcome.

Your spot in the woods, however large or small, should be enclosed with a fence—a fence that expresses the artistry, indeed the personality of the owner.   As for myself, I would choose the old rail fence because of my childhood memories.   In my boyhood days we held basket picnics next to the rail fence and the big elm tree.   Those were sweet experiences.   The spot was a sort of playground for nighborhood folks

SWANEE

both young and old. We'd meet at the big elm
next to the rail fence. And so rail fences warm
me. They belong to my youth. They belong to
me now. After all, rail fences are just as good
as any other kind of fence if you can get them.
They are simple to build. They have a sturdy,
homely dignity. I must admit I bought nearly
three-quarters of a mile of rail fence from a
farmer one time. He was tearing his fence
down. I bought it out of sentiment more than
actual need. I'm sure he must have said under
his breath, "They ain't worth cuttin' up for
firewood."

YANKEE

FRIENDLY TRAILS

Trails are plain paths or obscure windings among trees, rocks or boulders. They become more pronounced by use. Obscure trails are more intriguing. Step over a log or rock. Make your trail interesting, especially if it leads to your favorite hiding spot where you may want to be alone—away from the world. Or it may lead to your bird sanctuary or to a pet chipmunk who will come to you if you call and will eat from your hand.

You may want your trail to lead to a one-man shack, tucked away out of view. Put a small fireplace in the shack, a bunk, a book or two. Build it out of natural resources. Don't spend too much money. Go to it some starlit night. Take a friend in tune with your thinking. Here you will find the romance of "night, God and the Milky Way."

This may sound like a three hundred acre tract. No, I'm thinking of one, two or ten acres. Of course, if you are lucky enough to have more land, so much the better. Do you still have a farm belonging to the family from your childhood days? Don't let it get out of the family. Divide it, if need be, but hold on to it. Some day when you reach the age of forty, you will

wish you still had it, for just such a purpose as we are discussing. It has too many rich treasures and traditions to let it out of family hands. You will at some time in later years "revert back to the land."

To get back to trails, remember trails are undeveloped paths, not too obvious, not too clear-cut. Leave something to the imagination. "Shall we turn right or left? Now let's see . . . there are three stone markers, first a large one, then a smaller one and a still smaller one taking the shape of the point of an arrow." This is stalking.

Go alone. Sit by yourself and suddenly with God. If you have never done it, you will have a new experience. Birds will fly overhead. A chipmunk may chatter, a catydid may say his say and you will suddenly find yourself with God and at peace with the world. This is Christ in the mountains. You will find this a place for clear thinking on the eternal fitness of things.

So, my friend, your trail has not only led you to a place, but to a new opportunity; perhaps a challenge. Perhaps you will have really discovered yourself.

Great
Out
Doors

The

Great

Outdoors

OUR pioneer fathers learned the art of living happily together in God's outdoors. No running water. No electric lights. No radios. No automobiles. No servants. They lived simply —clear in thinking, clean in relationships, hard fighting, but friendly to a fault to a neighbor in distress. They lived by simple standards, asked little of life, were willing to work hard and contented with meager returns. Occasionally they relaxed. When they were playful they "played hard and when they worked they didn't play at all."

Life is different today. It's easier in many ways, but it is tense and highly geared. It plays on our nervous system. It does not contribute to wholesome fatigue at the end of a day as the fatigue of a day of simple hard labor—sweat, wholesome toil, physical things accomplished.

We of today have not changed much. Our environment has changed. We still have it in our blood to "revert to the land," to the out-of-doors. And just so, because of the pattern of city life, we need again to learn, as our fore-fathers did, the art of living happily together in the woods. In a word, going back somewhat to primitive thinking and living, simple pleasures, homely tasks. It calls for release from the urge of going to the movies, night clubs—late hours —continuous excitement as a steady diet—all of which is the result of restlessness and restless-ness is often the result of over-excitement and too much stimulation.

In our Cabin-in-the-Woods contentment may come from the quiet of friends around our fireside, neighborhood news, story telling, com-panionship, the enjoyment of a good book or unashamed we crawl into bed at the "ridicu-lous" hour of half past eight or nine o'clock.

Let us get still closer to the outdoors by liv-ing for a spell in a tent. Perhaps we can clar-ify a bit how we can come to better understand and enjoy the outdoors by a mere intimate knowledge and understanding of outdoor life, of the relationship of ourselves to the elements, to wild life, to those folks about us—simple living.

To live successfully out-of-doors, no matter if one is thirty, fifty or more, one needs a reasonable feeling of security. Added to this we need experience in outdoor living that will prove or disprove the things we have learned of the out-of-doors. Next, the urgent need of friendliness and understanding—friendliness with those about us, of wild animal life about us that brings happiness to us and security to them. Finally, we all need approval and satisfaction. Approval from those about us. Satisfaction in a job well done. To do so we need an outdoor setting. Will you and your family, therefore, go with me and mine to our favorite camp spot and camp in tents for a few days? Let's be primitive. It is June. New York State. Tents, duffel and equipment are all packed. A short thirty-mile trip and we are out in the woods; alone and away from the world. We have chosen the spot. Soon tents are up. The outdoor kitchen with pots, pans and improvised stove is all set. We are away for a long week-end on our own.

Now we must change from city togs to those of the out-of-doors. Let's be comfortable. A red shirt, colorful corduroy trousers or slacks shirt open at the neck.

This is lovely countryside. Nothing majestic, just rolling hills, valleys, trees, farms, fences—a small lake. We can see as our hillside slopes down to the small lake below scattered stately trees—elms, maples, especially one that stands alone and has spread its great branches, massive, proud, commanding. There are meadows about, bushes, young trees growing strong. Bushy trees shade our tents. The tree-stump nearby will serve as a feeding station for the squirrel and chipmunk playing hide and seek among the rocks and trees. See, they are looking us over. The spring-fed stream just beside our camp flows quietly. From the dugout pool comes a constant supply of sweet, fresh drinking water for our needs.

The small lake below us is fringed with trees. A few tents on the far side add contentment, for we know there, too, are lovers of the out-of-doors. Out of hearing distance, they add to the setting. A bright green upturned canoe on the sandy beach is clearly visible. The day is sunny and warm. Still. Serene.

Beyond the lake the land rises upward for several miles until it reaches the great skyline, dotted with trees, farms, forests. The hillside is laid out in great patches of farm lands, each surrounded by fences, some still with picturesque old-fashioned rail fences. Each plot is fringed with bushes, trees. To the right is the cow pasture—green—where contented cattle spend lazy long days. Far to the right is the great balsam swamp. We must make a trip there some day. It is really a bird sanctuary.

In the middle of all this setting is our neighboring farmer's house, barns, silos, garden spots and orchards. The "Moores" are hardworking folks. They live simply. They have no need to envy city folks. They are the salt of the earth and the backbone of our democracy.

So I welcome you to enjoy with me this lovely countryside.

Security

THE NORTH WOODS

Now that our camp is all set, let's sit down for a heart to heart talk. Let's talk about the art of living happily together in the woods.

What do we mean by "Security in the out-of-doors?" Is it self preservation, or it is accepting nature happily and living without mental reservations?

My daughter and I once made a canoe trip into Canadian waters. On arrival at a way-station we loaded our duffel into our canoe and paddled several miles down Pickerel River, stopping for breakfast with friends. It was raining hard. They wanted us to stay with them because of the wet weather. My daughter, after thanking them, turned to me and said, "Daddy, let's camp. We can take it." So we paddled on. We found an island to set up our camp and it became our island. We took one or two-day trips from our island camp. One day on returning we paddled nearly twenty miles. It was a

162

stormy rainy day. It was a hard pull against the strong head-wind. Late in the afternoon I said, "Sister, are you getting tired?" "No," she said and paddled on. I was grateful she didn't ask me. At last we found our island and our tent camp. We unloaded our duffel and dripping wet hurried to our tent. We quickly started a cheery reflector fire from dry wood stored within our tent. A change to dry linen, a good supper, and my daughter sat back and said, "Daddy, isn't this snug?" She was really saying she enjoyed the security of a companion who could "take it." Security in that great out-of-doors—miles from the nearest supply station and yet there we were happy, comfortable, with the feeling that we could take care of ourselves in those far-away primitive conditions and enjoy it. That is a bit of real security.

All of us who live in the woods need mental security. I wish I could by a miracle relieve all folks who through their childhood days had their lives spoiled by superstition, inhibitions, fears—those things that have gripped them and distorted their thinking because of misinformation. Do you still hesitate when a black cat crosses your path?

FEAR

I have been in many "tight" places in the Rockies and the Canadian woods and streams when fear gripped me to the point where mental processes ceased suddenly to be rational. Queer how environmental influence can play tricks with one's thinking.

Once while "shooting" swift rapids my canoe shipped water. The going was tough—"Can't make it"—fear—fright—then panic gripped me. "Help! Help!' But there was no one within miles. I pictured myself dead—stiff and cold at the bottom of the falls miles below. I hate water in my nose . . . My Last Will and Testament—What will happen to my new camping equipment?

This kind of thing comes with lightning speed. Fear grips you and strangles the ability to think sanely. Do something—attack and your fear begins to give way. Take a firm grip on your paddle and say over and over again, "I won't give up. I won't give up. I can make it. I will."

I've been lost on the trail. "The compass is 'cock-eyed.' It points the wrong way." I started to run. Crazy? Of course. You're really not lost. You're just confused. Get a hold on yourself. Sit down on a log. Put a cigarette between your teeth and look around. Gradually your tension lessens and normal thinking brings a returned faith in your compass and eventually the way back to the trail.

Fear keeps close companionship with doubt, flirts with mis-information, encourages lack of self-confidence, welcomes superstition, bogie-boos, inconsistency and goes hand in hand with worry. Fear is the hobgoblin of confused thinking. It comes from within. Grandmother used to say, "It's in you what ails you." I believe she's right. What ails you and what cures you are within you. Even night noises, stealthy footfalls, the panic of seeing a snake too suddenly—all met by thought or built into "mountains" by worry. "It's in you what ails you."

SNAKES

Suppose as we are sitting in our camp circle, I had "Uncle Benny," a big black seven-foot snake draped around my neck and stretched out on an extended arm. Gently stroking and petting his head (and he loved it) I walk over to you and say, "Here, will you take him?" How will you react? Let me tell you about "Uncle Benny." For several years in a camp for boys he was a pet of the entire camp. Twice a day they would take him in swimming—at eleven-thirty in the morning and five-thirty in the afternoon. Uncle Benny was temperamental and if he didn't get his swim on time, he would grow restless in his box and begin to squirm. You could almost set your watch by his re-actions. Believe it or not, we would take Uncle Benny out for a swim and had taught him to follow behind our canoe. After fifteen or twenty minutes he would come back with us and rest on the sandy shore and wait for some one to pick him up and take him back to his box. This was the prize experience in a day of ad-venture as some one would pick up that big black snake and carry him to his box. So we re-leased hundreds of campers from foolish fear that grips so many people. I am sure there must be a thousand photographs of Uncle Benny draped on somebody's shoulder. I must admit I have one of myself with him. This picture is in the family archives. Some day one of my great-grandchildren will view that picture and ac-cording to his training will label me a regular fellow or perhaps a bit "batty." While I do not wish to imply I love a snake as a bed fellow, nor do I recommend it, I no longer have foolish fears at the sight or touch of a black snake.

I must warn you, however, that it is wise to know your snakes. There are good and bad snakes, just as there are good and bad folks.

SKUNKS AND INSECTS

Let us try sleeping out on the grass in the open. Along about two o'clock in the morning, could you lie there peacefully, realizing suddenly that you had a visit from a skunk who sniffled all around you? A skunk is really one of the nicest little pets and has been unfairly accused over these years. He will come to your bed because he is just a curious fellow. He is getting acquainted and has the cutest little sniffle. After looking you over he will quietly amble off without harming you. I warn you, however, if you reach for a gun or an axe, the polecat will "shoot" first. Go to sleep, my friend, and feel secure in the thought that the polecat is your friend, too.

How many of us step on a spider as he crosses our path? Do we do it because we have added to God's great scheme of things and reduced the several billions of spiders by one? Or are we stepping on it in order to relieve some innate fear of ours—the fear that something might bite us? That's mental insecurity. I have known a mother whose little boy proudly showed her a great big toad which he carried in his hand. She stiffened, withdrew, tense—and gave him as his reward the assurance that he was going to have a handful of warts.

What I do want to say is that real security comes in the knowledge that "God is in his heaven" and has organized his great universe for our good. He has given you and me the privilege of being on it to enjoy it.

Years ago I met a man who had an uncanny dislike for mosquitoes, bugs, beetles and all creepy and crawling things. It was more than a dislike. He was fraught with fear. He termed them all insects—things unnecessary in the world—things to be despised. He was the product of misinformation in his early days. Then someone brought a change in his life. He met a naturalist in whom he had confidence. They sat on the grass on a dark night with several others. The naturalist lit a small candle and placed it in the damp grass, and said to the group as we circled about, "I'm going to show you a new world of insect life in which each has a purpose in the great scheme of the universe." We were fascinated. We forgot ourselves. With a long thin stick the naturalist pointed to each of the queer creatures as it crawled towards the light. A small bug crawled laboriously to the top of a blade of grass only to drop to the ground and then crawl up the next—always toward the light. Long spindly-legged mosquitoes hovered over the flame. June bugs harmlessly jumped and flew with a force past the candle and would stop with a thud against one of us. "Millers," moths would flit about. It was like going to a miniature circus or zoo. We were so deeply interested we did not even notice the hum of an occasional mosquito. Well, neither did our pioneer fathers.

My friend with all the fears and inhibitions had a rebirth and an understanding in which he became a part and accepted, at least in part, this wild life of the outdoors. He said finally, "It's all in the way you look at it." It gave him a mental readjustment, a new evaluation, released him from many foolish fears, gave him an added security and finally made him a decidedly better camping partner. This is not so easy to achieve in later life. Unless you, too, learn to accept this wild life, you will constantly be in conflict with yourself.

There are a squirrel and chipmunk flitting about our camp. They wonder who we are. Let's get acquainted. Put a bit of food on the nearby tree stump. The chipmunk will sneak up cautiously on the far side of the stump, blink one eye and seem to say, "Well, I'm going to try you out." The squirrel will grab his morsel and retire to a more secure spot, sit on his haunches and eat greedily while watching us. They are going to be our good friends before we get through with this camp; so will the birds and other wild life.

Experience

So much for security. Let us now discuss the value of experience in which we can prove the information we have been given as true, or possibly disprove the misinformation that comes from people who just do not know God's outdoors. True that "experience is a wonderful teacher," yet we must remember in dealing with the outdoors, nature is relentless and exacts a costly price for ignorance.

CAUTION

If camping on our own, obviously we must be our own "doctor, baker and candlestick maker." We must look after our own bodily needs and safety. If we are to enjoy our experience to the fullest, we must do all things based on correct information—but better still, on plain "horse sense," sound judgment.

Should we unwittingly drink from a stagnant pool of polluted water and discover during the night a bit of stomachache or even worse as the ditty goes, "If in heaven you awaken and find you were mistaken" we will never live to tell the rest of the world of our adventure. If you love to swim and swim out beyond your depth and endurance and find that you go under the water twice and can only come up once, your camping experience will not be in line with your plans and anticipation. Sound judgment must come into play in our every experience.

BAD JUDGMENT

Suppose you choose a lovely grassy spot down near a little babbling brook for your camp—a spot that looks like a perfect setting on a sunny day. You set up camp, pitch your tent, make up your bed, enjoy your campfire, retire and "wrap the draperies of your couch about you and lie down to pleasant dreams." Having gone to sleep, a quiet, slow drizzly rain starts to refresh the earth. But the overflow has been running down the hillside and into your little babbling brook. The waters have risen higher and higher—"stealing in on you like a thief in the night." Suddenly you have that embarrassing awakening to find the heaviest part of your anatomy quietly bathed by lapping waters from under your bed. So you grab your searchlight from under your pillow and have the added chagrin of finding that your shoes, your coffee, canned goods and underwear are playing hide and seek with each other as they float about within your tent. Pray God that tomorrow will be a sunny day because you will have to spend all of it drying out. I am pretty sure that next time you will set up your tent on higher ground. This knowledge one does not get out of books. It takes experience. This is applied education.

Then there is the camper who goes out to "rough it." He wants to be able to "take it." So with a little cotton blanket and minimum equipment he rolls out on the grass and goes blissfully to sleep. Along about two o'clock in the morning he finds that he is propped up on two "piers"—one nice little stone under his shoulder and one under his hips and he spends the next day nursing what he thinks may be lumbago. So he, too, will find the value of carefully preparing a good bed if he wants a good night's sleep. "Experience is a great teacher."

SUN WORSHIPPER

We next come to the sun worshipper—that person who loves to take a sun bath. Here again one learns from experience, for the sensitivity of one's skin determines the amount of sun he can take at a time. If the sky is a bit hazy, you can take the sun for one or more hours. Whereas a very brilliant direct ray of the sun may be so powerful that you can only stand it for fifteen minutes. With the proper oiling of the body, take a bit more next day until you become accustomed to the sunshine.

THE STORM KING

I wonder how many of us really love a storm? Are there some of us who still have fears and shrink from it? A storm is the refreshing variety in nature's program which leaves no possible monotony. More than this, it is real entertainment as the elements reveal their many moods. Light and color—ozone and refreshing fragrance—warmth and coolness. Swift shifting situations—changing moods and finally returning warmth of the sun. In the great scheme of things the earth has been refreshed—the world looks brighter—cleansed, sweet. We have had an added experience.

One of our group says as the sunny day wears on, "We are going to have a storm." The next person says, "How do you know? The day is clear and sunny." But the first person points out, "I see the smoke is hovering around the cabin over on the Moore farm. There is also a scurrying of wild animals, insects and flies are creeping up on the windward side of the trees and under-branches." Behold, we have a weather prophet in our midst. The countryside, the trails of the woods and skies are full of signs, signals and symbols.

Before long over the valley behind the Moore farmhouse there suddenly looms up a great big black cloud—moving swiftly upward and toward us. We see little flashes of lightning running up and down. Suddenly there is a deathly stillness about us. Clouds move faster; the earth suddenly changes in color to a delicate amber. Little gusts of wind swirl leaves about. The chipmunk scurries back and forth, and finally to his hiding place of security. The birds clear out of the sky and we hear the first crash of thunder. Hastily a robin makes her last flight with a big worm to feed those hungry mouths. There is another wild flash of lightning and a clap of thunder. Then someone points out that Mrs. Moore is hurriedly taking the washing from the clothes line. The rain storm is now a mile away.

It comes on relentlessly and with impending force. We tighten the ropes of our tent—for you always tighten a tent before a storm and loosen it when it rains. We move inside the tent flaps open. Again a dazzling flash of lightning, and accompanying thunder. It is deafening. Is there any one here now who would wrap his head in a towel and crawl under the bed and in that fear miss again and again through life one of the most beautiful experiences—the storm?

The earth is being washed and refreshed to the strains of God's great "symphony." A jagged flash of lightning tears the black storm-clouds open—followed by a crash of "cymbals" and the beat of a thousand "kettle drums." Then the wind in varying moods plays majestically on thousands upon ten thousands of "violins."

We hear the first light patter of rain-drops on our tent; then a steady rhythm followed by a hard-driving rain. We sit comfortably and secure inside our tent enjoying this great experience. The world has grown dark. The little stream near our tent has developed from a mere trickle into a gurgling brook, and finally into a rushing little "torrent." The landscape has faded to a dull misty gray.

I know of a mother who once said to her child in a situation like this, "God must be very angry." How stupid. This is God's Out Doors.

The storm passes on. The rain abates. Then comes that moment of tremendous quiet. I can not describe it. You have got to live through it—that moment when there is hardly a sound in the world it seems, except the little stream before us that says, "Gurgle, gurgle, gurgle." And the quiet drops from rain-drenched leaves. Finally the squirrel comes out of his hiding place. Bird life appears. The storm has washed the earth. Overhead the gray sky is shifting, moving restlessly about. It forms into many-shaped clouds. Suddenly there is a rift in the sky and it seems you can look a "million" miles into the great blue void beyond. "God is in his heaven." Are we going to have a sunset? Sure enough. Back of us the clouds shift and open up as brilliant colors of the sun cast a ray across the valley and upon the Moore farm, transforming it into that lovely picture of our childhood days, "The House of Golden Windows."

NIGHT ENCHANTMENT

Supper over and the campfire. Eyes focused upon the flames. We are drawn closer together. Confidences are shared and friends are in tune. Cooling embers. The moon overhead. Enchantment. A longing. "Time to retire," something within says. Let us pause. A last smoke. Drink deep of the night as we look at the stars—the great beyond. Have you ever really looked searchingly at the stars? Have you really gazed and studied long enough to see not only one million, but two, three and more millions of twinkling stars—so many, so myriad that finally there is no room in the sky because of them? Do this. Do it long and do it searchingly and you will realize again and again that "God is in His heaven."

THE BURSTING SPLENDOR OF SUNRISE

After a night's refreshing sleep there is no sweeter awakener than the morning sunrise of many colors. I love sunrise because it brings a new day, a new opportunity, a new world. Rising early you will feel refreshed and wide awake. You will discover a peace of mind, relaxed muscles and suddenly an urge to get up and about, and do things. You warm yourself twice—first by cutting your firewood which loosens muscles and stirs the blood. Then you warm yourself in front of your fireplace, campfire or kitchen stove. The sweet smell of frying bacon, the rich aroma of coffee and finally a "royal" breakfast.

Where is the morning paper full of stock markets, murders, war, births, deaths? Well, sit back, Mr. Cabin-Builder, and enjoy your breakfast. Let the world go by. No radio? Tune your ears to the song of the birds and wild life about you. A cricket may chirp on your hearth. You will find the stillness most restful.

The sun is now over the horizon—many brilliant colors—shifting shadows. It is morning—early morning and a new day. This indeed is a different world.

THE MASTER PAINTER

The morning wears on and as the heat of the sun bathes the earth, we see a humid shimmer rising sunward to form new clouds and to carry out the great scheme of the universe in its regular succession of creation. Birds fly lazily across the sky. Animal life appears to be taking nature in its stride. The flying of birds across the sun is no longer ornithology, it is religion. God's Out Doors.

Great white banks of stately clouds, one after the other, move across the sky. The "Master Painter" with a bold stroke with each passing cloud swabs the earth, changing it from brilliant greens, reds, purples to soft pastels, only to quietly and quickly change them back to brilliant hues, and to repeat and repeat the process.

Security based on correct information, and experience based on true facts, will give us the appreciation that God has placed us in a beautiful world. It can and will bring us peace and happiness.

Friendliness

What is sweeter in life than friendliness? If there is any place in the world that will produce friendliness and kindliness it is the out-of-doors. Did you ever have that rich experience of sleeping in a tent with a buddy who got up quietly in the morning without disturbing you, rebuilt the campfire of the night before and started the day's program? After reheating the double-boiler of porridge that had been steaming all night, instead of saying to you, "Get up, old man, don't expect me to do all the work," he waits until the aroma of cooking bacon and coffee waft their way toward you. Suddenly you arouse, stretch your arms and say, "Why I have only slept ten minutes." You have really slept like a child and here your friend has added to your happiness in getting the breakfast. So down to the creek to make your toilet; back refreshed and then to do justice to an unrationed appetite. Describe and do it justice? Who can? You must live through it.

The chipmunk on the nearby stump where you placed food cautiously steals up, blinks one of his little bright eyes at you and seems to say,

"I like your friendliness." Birds come down to your feeding station—perhaps a bit cautious at first, but they come. Having been served a "royal" breakfast, you now will want to take your share of the load by cleaning up camp. If on a hike your partner develops a sore toe or blister, you say with nonchalance, "Give me your pack. I'll carry it." That's friendliness.

The trail in the woods is friendly. One does not stalk with heavy feet through the woods, but with the lithe toe-and heel tread of the Indian so as not to disturb the wild-life. Go through the woods lightly and with music in your heart. As you trail through the woods you will be amazed to find that nature is full of "signs, signals and symbols." These, too, are friendly signs if you can read them. True you will find no highway marked "Route 20," but every trail is marked equally effective by Mother Nature. There are signs that tell you a spring is near; where to find food; of approaching storms. We need only to learn them, to find that nature is friendly and eager to tell us through her method of signs and symbols how to enjoy wild life. She guards her secrets from those who treat them lightly, but gives of them willingly to those who study her ways.

Approval

Now we come to the most important part of our discussion—the need for a right attitude toward life; a balanced understanding of what brings security to us. Out of that friendliness built through experience one with another, comes the very foundation of the good life. No four people could go up into the wilds of Canada and live for a week or more together and have one of the four a "drone." Each must carry his share of the load. National wealth comes out of honest hard labor and effort of the individual "to earn a little and to spend a little less." Somehow in our cities there creeps into our communal life poachers, parasites, people who live off of other people. They contribute little to the world, but in the great outdoors, in this whole field of friendliness, comes this conception of building a democracy. The desire of one to do a little more than his share to add to the happiness of the group.

I have seen over and over when a group of six or eight boys camp together, one will be selfish, self-centered, stingy, greedy. After a period of a week or two in the woods with his buddies, he comes back a changed person. It may mean a bloody nose. The treatment may be a bit severe from his peers, but he will finally carry his share of the load if he has the fortitude to "take it" and stand by. Then some day one of the boys will make up his bed and he will come in and say, "Who has been monkeying with my bed?" The next lad will say, "Well, you carried in wood today and I sort of thought I would help you out." Something tremendous is happening to this selfish lad. It will take a day or two before he will do a kindness in return, but before the camp is over he will give a good account of himself. When he returns home he may say to his father, "Do you mind if I cut the lawn today?" Father may ask mother, "Is that boy sick?" No, he has just learned to carry his share of the load.

If you were to say to me, "Buddy, you can broil the best steaks in the world," I'd just swell up and love it, and I'd try harder to justify that approval you have given me. You know what I mean by the glow that comes to you when someone slaps you on the back and says, "You did the job swell. You conducted an inspiring campfire." Recognition comes from our friends who not only approve of us, but in the approving indicate that they think well of us. In modern slang we hear, "He is a good egg. He is the kind who can take it on the chin. A regular fellow."

To be in tune with the outdoors you must have a song in your heart and the song gives its own approval. Perhaps the most material proof that you are a "regular fellow" comes from the little chipmunk on the stump, who no longer pays any attention to you—has taken you in as a part of the woods—and the squirrel overhead no longer scolds, but accepts you—the birds that come to your feeding stations and pay no attention; when your friends like to be with you, not because of your money, not because of your influence or any possible superior advantage or abilities, but just because you are you—a balanced individual—a regular fellow.

When you merit all these the world will salute you as a master camper, a partner, a friend. You have learned the art of living happily together with folks, with nature, with wildlife in the woods. Most of all, you have learned to live comfortably with yourself.